Penguin Handbooks

SUZY COOKSTRIP

Suzy Benghiat writes:

'I was born and brought up in Egypt of a British father and Italian mother – both of Spanish Sephardic origin. I came to Britain in 1948 and worked for the BBC French Service as a bilingual secretary and then with French radio and television in London as production assistant. In 1968 I started freelancing in television production and radio journalism. By background and temperament I am a cosmopolitan and interested in people's customs, tastes, ways of life and their food, which is an important part of their cultural heritage. I have travelled extensively in France, Italy, Yugoslavia and Jamaica.'

Peter Maddocks writes:

'Born in Birmingham on April the First in the same year as Mickey Mouse. Ran away to sea at the age of fifteen and travelled around the world for five magical years. Came ashore for the love of a woman and started writing Kit Carson stories for comic books, progressed to cartooning for newspapers via Fleet Street, and the *Daily Sketch*. Ran a strip cartoon called Four D. Jones in the *Daily Express* for ten years. Now work from my own studio in Fleet Street, selling my work to the *Daily Mirror*, *Sunday Express*, *Evening News* and *Mayfair* magazine, syndicated around the world. Formed the London School of Cartooning Ltd, the first British all-cartooning correspondence school. Founded the British Cartoonist Association. Love skateboarding.'

In 1975–6 Suzy Benghiat and Peter Maddocks published *Sally Cookstrip*, a weekly feature in *Woman's Realm*, which forms the basis of this book.

SUZY BENGHIAT AND
PETER MADDOCKS

SUZY COOKSTRIP

PENGUIN BOOKS

For Monique
and in loving memory
of my mother to whom
I owe it all.

S.B.

For the person who
invented the fibretip
pen.

P.M.

Penguin Books Ltd, Harmondsworth,
Middlesex, England
Penguin Books, 625 Madison Avenue,
New York, New York 10022, U.S.A.
Penguin Books Australia Ltd, Ringwood,
Victoria, Australia
Penguin Books Canada Ltd, 2801 John Street,
Markham, Ontario, Canada L3R 1B4
Penguin Books (N.Z.) Ltd, 182–190 Wairau Road,
Auckland 10, New Zealand

Published in Penguin Books 1978

Made and printed in Great Britain by
Richard Clay (The Chaucer Press) Ltd
Bungay, Suffolk

contents

acknowledgements

I wish to thank all those who have helped me with tips, recipes and ideas, particularly my aunt, Mary Hayon, for being the depositary of our family tradition; my sister-in-law, Norma Benghiat, for her Jamaican cooking; Manoli Yustos, for our lively discussions and exchange of ideas while she cuts and sets my hair; my friend, Simone Savlié, for her rich repertoire of sweets and cakes; my colleague at the BBC, Eliane Matalon, an enthusiastic cook who selflessly gave me the results of her experimentation (I owe to her the substitution of turnip for aubergine on page 105). And of course I wish to thank my niece, Monique, for being my most enthusiastic guinea-pig and critic.

I would like to acknowledge my debt to the cookery writers who have given me inspiration and pleasure: Tante Marie; Elizabeth David, for her beautiful writing and the obvious pleasure she takes in cooking; Dharamjit Singh, for introducing me to the delights of Indian cooking; Jane Grigson, who makes the claim for an English cookery tradition believable and tempting to explore, and last but not least my friend Claudia Roden, for all the qualities which have made her famous, but most of all for the warm nostalgia which overtakes me every time I open *Middle Eastern Food*.

Peter and I wish to thank Veronica Bird who, as editor of *Woman's Realm*, gave us our first exposure by publishing in 1975–6 a weekly feature of our strip under the title of 'Sally Cookstrip', out of which this book evolved.

I owe a great debt to Pat and Lorraine Maddocks, Peter's wife and daughter for their help and encouragement in 'previewing' each strip before we sent it in to *Woman's Realm*. Their constructive criticism and their compliments were invaluable in testing whether the strip 'worked' in practice.

We are grateful to Jill Norman of Penguin Books for having seen the possibilities of such an unconventional cookery book and to Felicia Pheasant, our editor, for all her friendly and efficient help.

INTRODUCTION

SUZY'S LOVE OF FOOD STARTED IN EGYPT WHERE SHE GREW UP. HER COSMOPOLITAN UPBRINGING INTRODUCED HER TO ALL SORTS OF CUISINE; FRENCH, ITALIAN JEWISH, ARABIC, INDIAN, JAMAICAN AND OF COURSE ENGLISH

WHY DON'T I WRITE A BOOK ABOUT FOOD? ...I DON'T WANT TO WRITE A CONVENTIONAL RECIPE BOOK. I'D RATHER LIKE TO DO SOMETHING MORE FLEXIBLE

I'M A BETTER CARTOONIST THAN I AM A COOK— THESE COOKSTRIPS I'M WORKING ON MAY LOOK OK BUT THE RECIPES ARE AWFUL

SUZY—JUST THE PERSON I WANT, I'M STRUGGLING WITH A COOKSTRIP IDEA BUT I NEED A GREAT COOK

I'M WRITING A COOKBOOK MYSELF, PETER SO WHY DON'T WE GET TOGETHER AND PRODUCE SOMETHING NEW AND ORIGINAL?

I ALWAYS TALK TO MYSELF WHEN I'M COOKING SO THE FIRST THING TO DO IS TO RECORD EVERY WORD I SAY
BLAST! IT'S DRYING UP—I NEED MORE WATER
I'LL TYPE EVERYTHING OUT AND TAKE IT ROUND TO PETER
CHATTER CHATTER
IT TOOK ME HOURS TO WRITE THIS OUT AND YOU CAN SUM IT UP IN ONE OR TWO PICTURES
SUZY, THE WAY YOU DESCRIBE IT I CAN PRACTICALLY TASTE IT
THESE ARE GREAT —WHAT OTHER KINDS OF DISHES ARE WE GOING TO INCLUDE?
EVERYTHING YOU WOULD FIND IN SUZY'S KITCHEN CHEAP DISHES, EXPENSIVE ONES, LIGHT, RICH, SIMPLE, COMPLICATED, FROM ALL OVER THE WORLD

UNLESS SUZY TELLS YOU OTHERWISE ALL THE RECIPES GIVE ENOUGH FOOD FOR **4** PEOPLE

SOUPS

- IT'S AMAZING HOW COOKING DEVELOPS & EXTENDS THE RANGE OF YOUR TASTES...
- I FOR INSTANCE NEVER LIKED SOUP UNTIL I STARTED COOKING
- I NOW LOVE IT & ENJOY CREATING NEW BLENDS AND A FEW BASIC IDEAS...

CHICKEN BROTH

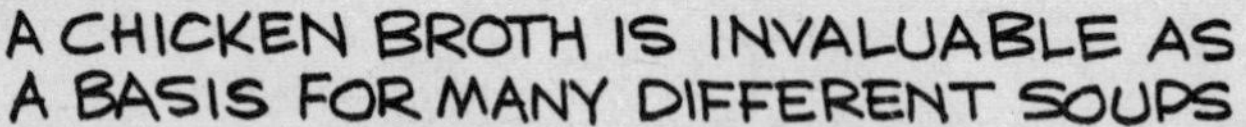

A CHICKEN BROTH IS INVALUABLE AS A BASIS FOR MANY DIFFERENT SOUPS

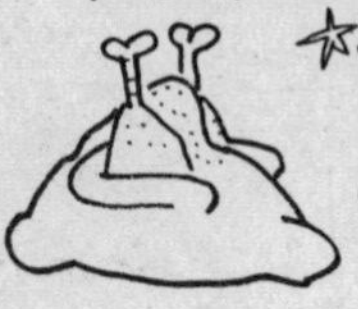

☆ TAKE A BOILING CHICKEN

OR A PACKET OF FROZEN GIBLETS WHICH YOU CAN GET FROM MOST SUPERMARKETS

COLD WATER TO COVER

BRING SLOWLY TO BOILING POINT & LET IT SIMMER

SKIM OFF ALL THE FROTH AS IT APPEARS

ADD: A LARGE CARROT
AN ONION

CUT UP A CELERY STICK
2 BAY LEAVES SALT & PEPPER

LOWER HEAT—
LET IT SIMMER FOR A GOOD 2 HOURS
(OR ½ hr IN A PRESSURE COOKER)
THEN REMOVE CHICKEN...

(WHICH CAN THEN BE COOKED IN DIFFERENT WAYS SEE PAGES: 130, 131.)

AFTER ANOTHER HOUR'S SIMMERING —
STRAIN THE BROTH INTO A BOWL
& REMOVE FAT

IF YOU KEEP THE BOWL IN THE FRIDGE—ANY REMAINING FAT WILL SOLIDIFY ON THE SURFACE & WILL BE EASY TO REMOVE

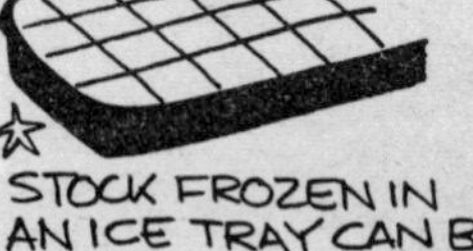

☆ STOCK FROZEN IN AN ICE TRAY CAN BE KEPT IN A BAG IN THE FREEZER

CREAM OF TOMATO SOUP

LEEK & POTATO CREAM SOUP

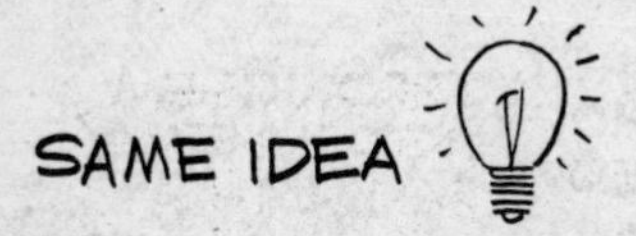

SAME METHOD

* DIFFERENT INGREDIENTS
* DIFFERENT FLAVOURS

(1) ONE LARGE ONION
ONE LARGE CUCUMBER
+ CLOVE OF GARLIC

(2) ONE LARGE OR MEDIUM LETTUCE (SHREDDED)
1lb SHELLED PEAS

(3) ONE MEDIUM ONION
GARLIC
3lb MUSHROOMS

* COOKED SLOWLY WITH A GOOD LUMP OF BUTTER & STOCK – LIQUIDISE & SERVE AS FOLLOWS:

1. CHILL & SERVE WITH YOGURT & CHOPPED MINT
2. SERVE WITH FRESH CREAM & CHOPPED GREEN PARTS OF A SPRING ONION
3. SERVE WITH CREAM & CHOPPED PARSLEY

FRENCH ONION SOUP

PREPARE AN OVEN PROOF DISH WITH STALE TOASTED BREAD
(GOOD BREAD – NOT THE PLASTIC VARIETY)

CUBES OF CHEESE & BUTTER

POUR THE SOUP OVER IT — A GLASS OF DRY SHERRY IN THE SOUP WOULD MAKE IT EXTRA SPECIAL

SPRINKLE WITH GRATED CHEESE AND POP INTO A MEDIUM HOT OVEN FOR ABOUT 20 MINUTES OR UNTIL THE TOP IS CRUSTY & GOLDEN

LENTIL SOUP

GOSH—WHAT A NIGHT JUST THE WEATHER FOR A RICH SOUP
BRRRRRR
I'VE GOT ABOUT ½ lb OF Lentils AND THIS NICE PIECE OF BACON KNUCKLE + 1 ONION AND ONE CLOVE OF GARLIC
Lentils
SORT OUT THE LENTILS
THEY USED TO BE FULL OF STONES & THINGS— NOW YOU ONLY FIND THE ODD BIT TO DISCARD!
RINSE LENTILS
Meanwhile... I FRY THE CHOPPED ONION AND GARLIC
THEN I ADD 1 TEASPOON OF CUMIN POWDER
THIS IS WHAT GIVES THIS SOUP A DISTINCTIVE FLAVOUR
Quickly— SOME WATER BEFORE IT BURNS
NOW ADD: THE Lentils THE BACON
MORE WATER TO COVER: ABOUT 2" OVER
BRING TO THE BOIL LOWER THE Heat cover & Simmer
ABOUT 45 MINUTES
LOW HEAT
AFTER ABOUT ½ hour...
OH DEAR—ALL THE WATER'S GONE— I'LL ADD SOME MORE
What an Aroma
REMOVE KNUCKLE & LIQUIDISE
BACK INTO THE PAN—ADD SALT & TASTE
IT'S LOVELY AND THICK SERVE WITH CROÛTONS & A BLOB OF BUTTER...
TO MAKE CROÛTONS
BUTTER THICK SLICES OF BREAD
THEN CUT THEM INTO CUBES
NOW POP INTO THE OVEN UNTIL NICE AND CRISP
I PREFER THIS METHOD TO FRYING: IT'S MORE ECONOMICAL ON BUTTER:- and Calorie wise!

*VARIATIONS:
WITH DIFFERENT PULSES

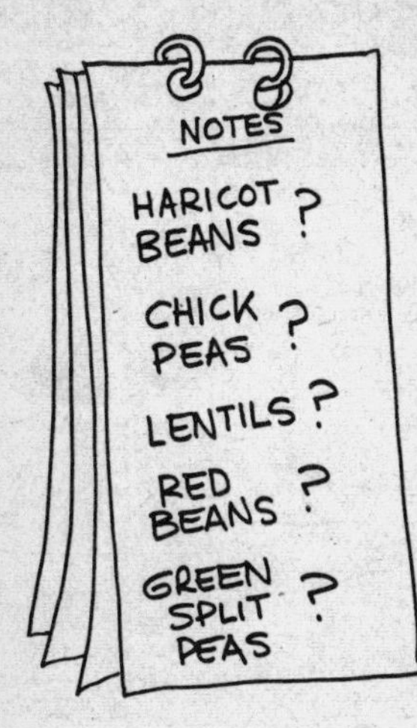

Hmm FOR FLAVOUR
I ALSO HAVE A CHOICE

FRESH HERBS LIKE
TARRAGON & MINT
BASIL OR PARSLEY
OR DIFFERENT
SPICES

—BUT THE BEST WAY TO DECIDE ON THE FLAVOURING, ONCE THE SOUP IS MADE, IS TO EXPERIMENT WITH SMALL QUANTITIES — TASTE, ADJUST, TASTE AGAIN & ADOPT!

MINESTRONE SOUP

VARIATIONS

★ INSTEAD OF THE BACON STRIPS I SOMETIMES USE A HAM KNUCKLE

A GOOD BROTH OR EVEN A COUPLE OF STOCK CUBES

★ IF YOU MUST HAVE PASTA —

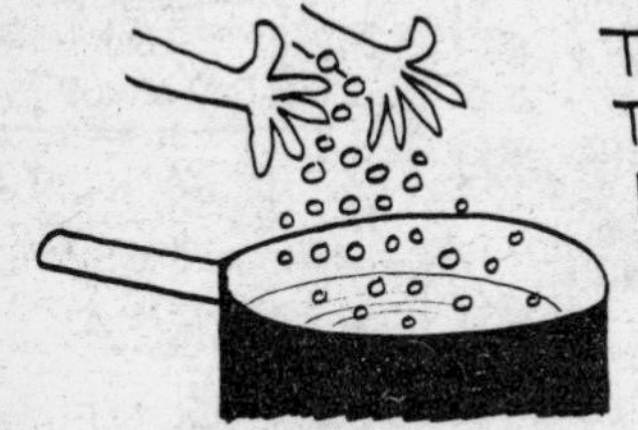

THROW IT INTO THE SOUP ABOUT 10 MINUTES BEFORE SERVING

(YOU MIGHT NEED TO ADD WATER TO THE SOUP)

★ IF YOU ARE LUCKY ENOUGH TO HAVE FRESH BASIL CHOP SOME & ADD TO THE SOUP BEFORE SERVING

AAHHH... BASIL...

EGG & LEMON CHICKEN SOUP

STRACCIATELLA

STARTERS
SALADS

THREE PARTY DIPS

③ I CAN TELL YOU —I MADE TWO OF THESE DIPS
④ FIRST I SQUASH THE BLUE CHEESE
⑤ 2oz
ROQUEFORT
GORGONZOLA
OR
DANISH

⑨ Mmm IT'S GREAT EATEN WITH
CELERY
I MADE THE OTHER DIP IN THE SAME WAY BUT INSTEAD OF BLUE CHEESE I USED — WAIT FOR IT...
A PACKET OF ONION SOUP
SOUP
JUST LIKE THAT?
YES— THAT'S THE SECRET!

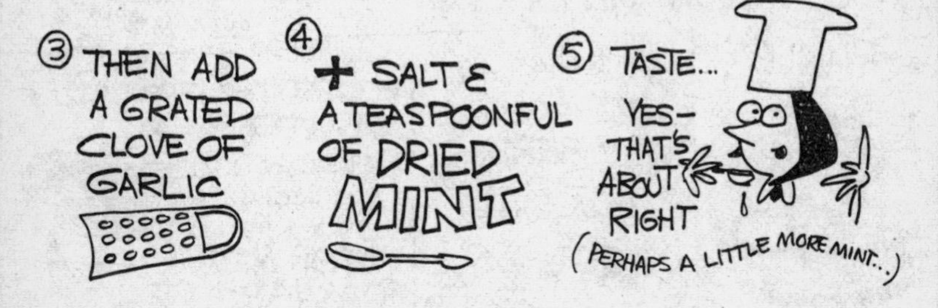

③ THEN ADD A GRATED CLOVE OF GARLIC
④ + SALT & A TEASPOONFUL OF DRIED MINT
⑤ TASTE...
YES— THAT'S ABOUT RIGHT
(PERHAPS A LITTLE MORE MINT...)

AUBERGINE PUREÉ

GREEN AND/OR RED PEPPER SALAD

GRILL PEPPERS IN THE SAME WAY AS AUBERGINE UNTIL SKIN IS ALL 'BLISTERED'...

PLACE IN A BOWL COVERED WITH A CLOTH FOR ABOUT TEN MINUTES

IT WILL MAKE THE PEELING EASY

PEEL

CUT INTO STRIPS

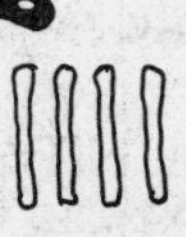

AND DISCARD SEEDS

SPRINKLE WITH GRATED GARLIC, SALT, VINEGAR & CHOPPED PARSLEY

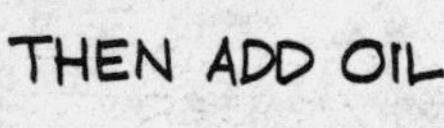

THEN ADD OIL

CHICKEN LIVER MOUSSE

* I'VE ALSO TRIED THIS MOUSSE WITH CALVES' LIVER BUT THE FLAVOUR WAS A BIT TOO STRONG...

SO I BEAT A SMALL CARTON OF DOUBLE CREAM INTO IT AND ADDED A SPOONFUL OF BRANDY —

WHAT A DISCOVERY!

TO ME A SALAD IS
MANY THINGS...
AN HORS-D'OEUVRE
IT CAN ACCOMPANY A
MAIN COURSE OR CAN
COME AFTER IT...
BUT IT NEVER, NEVER IS

A LIMP PIECE
OF LETTUCE,
3 TRANSPARENT
SLICES OF
CUCUMBER,
A SWEATY SLICE
OF BEETROOT,
A ROCK HARD
BOILED EGG
+ ONE TIRED SPRING ONION + A LUMP OF MAYONNAISE

- I'M VERY CONSERVATIVE ABOUT THE DRESSING I USE... SALT, LIME, (IF POSSIBLE, OTHERWISE LEMON) PEPPER & OIL (IN THAT ORDER)

- I LIKE TO ADD SOME FRESH OR DRIED HERBS (MINT IS PARTICULARLY NICE OR EVEN A SPRINKLE OF SPICES)

SOME OF MY FAVOURITES

EGYPTIAN SALAD:

COS LETTUCE
CUT UP VERY SMALL
CUCUMBER CUT INTO
SMALL CUBES
TOMATOES ALSO
CUT VERY SMALL
+ THE DRESSING

LOVELY WITH KEBAB, GRILLED MEATBALLS, WITH RICE, (IT GETS IMPREGNATED WITH ALL THE JUICES) & BELIEVE IT OR NOT — WITH HAGGIS
(I GOT THIS TIP FROM A SCOTTISH FRIEND)

MUSHROOM SALAD AS FIRST COURSE

SLICE THE RAW MUSHROOMS
ADD DRESSING AN HOUR OR
SO BEFORE SERVING AND
SPRINKLE WITH PARSLEY.

* & A FINELY CHOPPED
CLOVE OF GARLIC

COLE SLAW:

SHREDDED CABBAGE

SPRINKLED WITH SALT
COVER WITH A PLATE
& WEIGHT DOWN

* AFTER A COUPLE OF HOURS
IT WILL BE SOFT.

PRESS THE LIQUID
OUT THEN ADD THE
REST OF THE
DRESSING + A
PINCH OF CUMIN
POWDER

RELISHES

* A COUPLE OF EXAMPLES OF RELISHES TO EAT WITH AN INDIAN MEAL (PAGE 135)

  WITH KEBAB OR GRILLED MEATBALLS

* YOU CAN ALSO ADD SMALL DISHES OF MANGO CHUTNEY AND PICKLED LIME (THESE CAN BE BOUGHT)

① MARINATED ONIONS

FINELY SLICED ONIONS
SPRINKLE WITH SALT
& VINEGAR
LEAVE FOR AT LEAST
A COUPLE OF HOURS
ADD OIL & CAYENNE
PEPPER

② YOGURT & MINT

BEAT A SMALL
CARTON OF YOGURT
ADD TABLESPOON OF
DRIED MINT, SALT &
A SPRINKLE OF
CAYENNE PEPPER

* SOMETIMES I LIKE TO COMBINE BOTH

③ AN EGYPTIAN SALAD (PAGE 27)

PITTA BREAD

1 TABLESPOON OF SALT
1 lb STRONG WHITE PLAIN FLOUR
½ PINT TEPID WATER
DISSOLVE ½ OZ FRESH OR ¼ OZ DRIED YEAST IN SOME OF THE TEPID WATER FROM THE JUG
POUR THE YEAST MIXTURE + THE WATER INTO THE WELL & MIX
FLOUR
MAKE A WELL IN THE CENTRE
FLOURED BOARD
KNEAD THE DOUGH FOR A GOOD 10 MINS. UNTIL ELASTIC & SILKY TO TOUCH
PUT A GOOD TABLESPOON OF OIL INTO THE BOWL AND TURN THE DOUGH INTO IT
COVER WITH A CLOTH & LEAVE TO PROVE
SET OVEN AT 475
GAS MARK 9
GOOD IT HAS MORE THAN DOUBLED ITS SIZE
(IT TAKES ABOUT 2 HOURS IN AN AIRING CUPBOARD — BUT LONGER OUTSIDE...)
TAKE IT OUT AND KNEAD FOR ABOUT 1 MINUTE...
TAKE A PIECE OF DOUGH THE SIZE OF AN EGG...
NOW FLATTEN IT INTO AN OVAL
7"
YOU GET ABOUT 12
PLACE THEM ON A TEA-TOWEL ON TOP OF THE COOKER...
NOW- THE OVEN IS HOT
WARM UP AN OILED BAKING SHEET (5 MINS)
TRANSFER LOAVES TO HOT BAKING SHEET AND POP INTO OVEN FOR ABOUT 15 MINS.
THEY'LL "SWELL" AS THEY COOK
WHEN COOL CUT OPEN LIKE A POUCH AND FILL WITH ANYTHING YOU LIKE Kebabs Salad HAMBURGERS HAM etc... etc. etc.

FOR A SPECIAL FLAVOUR...

TRY MIXING ¼ lb OF RYE FLOUR TO ¾ lb OF WHITE FLOUR PLUS A TEASPOON OF CUMIN POWDER

(AND THEN FOLLOW PREVIOUS RECIPE)

THE PITTA BREAD KEEPS VERY WELL IN THE FRIDGE & BETTER STILL IN THE FREEZER

TAKE OUT & POP INTO PRE-HEATED OR VERY HOT GRILL FOR A MINUTE OR SO — TURN OVER & YOU'LL SEE THEY'LL SWELL AGAIN
I ALWAYS DO THIS WITH BOUGHT PITTA TOO!

LIGHT
MAIN
DISHES

...OR
FIRST
COURSES

SHORT PASTRY (SAVOURY)...

①

②

THIS IS ESPECIALLY EASY TO MAKE EVEN IF YOU HAVE NO SCALES

⑥

POUR IT INTO A MIXING BOWL

⑦

POUR IT INTO THE BUTTER & REFILL WITH SAME AMOUNT OF WATER...

WHICH ALSO GOES INTO THE BOWL

* ADD ONE TABLESPOON OF SALT

⑪

WHEN THE DOUGH COMES OFF THE SIDES OF THE BOWL YOU TAKE IT WITH YOUR HAND

⑫

⑮

ONCE YOU'VE GOT THE HANG OF IT— IT TAKES ONLY A FEW MINUTES

☆ ABOUT THE TIME IT TAKES TO GET A READY MADE PASTRY OUT OF ITS WRAPPING

⑯

WITH THIS RECIPE YOU NEVER NEED TO FLOUR OR BUTTER THE DISH OR TRAY

A STEP BY STEP GUIDE

④ POUR THE MELTED BUTTER INTO A SMALL CUP

⑤ IT JUST ABOUT FILLS THIS COFFEE CUP

⑩ AT THE BEGINNING IT'S LIKE STIRRING A SAUCE — THEN GRADUALLY IT TURNS INTO A DOUGH
IT SHOULD TAKE ABOUT

½lb FLOUR

⑬ NOW IT'S READY TO USE — BUT YOU CAN ALSO LEAVE IT IN THE FRIDGE OR FREEZER LIKE...

⑱ SAVOURY TARTS & QUICHES

QUICHE & SAVOURY TARTS (LARGE OR SMALL)

A PASTRY BASE...

* SHORT OR PUFF
* **PRE-COOKED OR UNCOOKED**
* HOME MADE OR BOUGHT
* WITH VARIOUS FILLINGS

FILLINGS THREE EXAMPLES

① QUICHE LORRAINE (FOR 8/10 OZ PASTRY)

FRY FIVE OR SIX RASHERS OF BACON CUT UP SMALL
(NO SALT AS THE BACON IS SALTY)

2 EGGS & ½ PINT OF CREAM

WHISK & POUR INTO **UNCOOKED** PASTRY

ADD BACON PIECES

COOK FOR ABOUT 1 HOUR IN **HOT** OVEN

---

② ON PRE-COOKED INDIVIDUAL TARTLETS

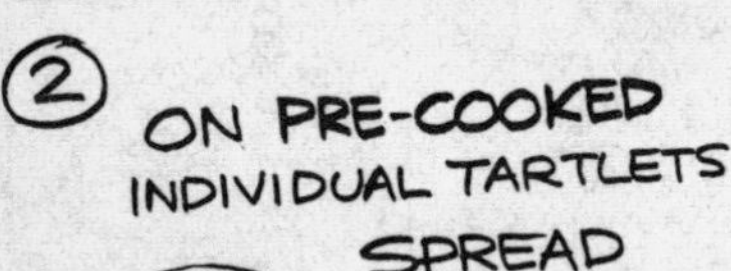

SPREAD TOMATO SAUCE
(PAGE 74)

ADD SLICES OF FRIED AUBERGINE
TOP WITH THIN SLICES OF CHEESE
POP UNDER HOT GRILL

---

③ BEAT 2 EGGS & GRATED CHEESE IN A SMALL BOWL OF LEFT OVER RATATOUILLE
(PAGE 58)

SPREAD ON A PIE SHELL PRE-COOKED OR UNCOOKED
(½ HOUR / 1 HOUR)

THIS WILL MAKE A NICE DISH FOR 4

SPINACH QUICHE

☆ VARIATIONS WITH MUSHROOMS

SAUTÉ SOME SLICED MUSHROOMS IN BUTTER
COOK UNTIL JUICES ARE REDUCED

MIX WITH BÉCHAMEL (PAGE 78)

AND CONTINUE AS ON OPPOSITE PAGE

OR WITH ONIONS

SAUTÉ THE ONIONS IN BUTTER
WHEN GOLDEN MIX WITH THE BÉCHAMEL ETC.

CHEESE & SPINACH PIE

* ALTHOUGH I CHOP THE SPINACH I PREFER TO HAVE IT IN LEAF FORM AT FIRST SINCE CHOPPED BOUGHT SPINACH IS MUCH TOO WATERY

* TRY IT WITH A MEAT FILLING...

BROWN 6oz MINCED MEAT & CHOPPED ONION

FLAVOUR WITH NUTMEG & CHOPPED PARSLEY...

BEAT IN 2 EGGS

* FILL THE PASTRY AS ON OPPOSITE PAGE

SMALL CHEESE PASTIES

TRY THIS UNUSUAL FILLING

SOFTEN 1 LARGE CHOPPED ONION IN SOME OIL... WHEN DARK GOLD ADD:

ONE LARGE AUBERGINE (CUT INTO CUBES OR SLICES) ONE MEDIUM TIN OF PEELED TOMATOES

SALT & PEPPER & SIMMER UNTIL THE WHOLE THING BECOMES A MUSH AND DRIES OUT

STIR FROM TIME TO TIME TO AVOID BURNING AND SCRAPE PAN IF NECESSARY

COOL IN A BOWL

THEN POUR OUT EXCESS OIL (IF ANY)

AND FILL THE PASTIES

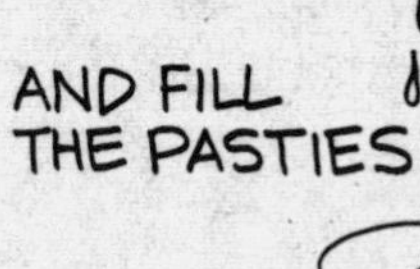

JAMAICAN BEEF PATTIES

*VARIATION WITH VEGETABLE FILLING

THROW IN:

DICED POTATOES
& CARROTS
PEAS
BARELY COVER
WITH WATER—
SALT, PEPPER
& CURRY POWDER*

COVER PAN: TOSS FROM TIME TO TIME UNTIL COOKED
(IT SHOULDN'T TAKE MORE THAN HALF AN HOUR)

*TRY OWN MIXTURE — PAGE 114

PANCAKE BATTER

④ NOW ADD 4 TABLESPOONS OF MELTED BUTTER
ABOUT 2OZ
⑤ TRY NOT TO GET ANY LUMPS —IF YOU DO SIEVE THE MIXTURE
⑥ BUT WITH AN ELECTRIC BLENDER YOU WON'T NEED TO
(JUST THROW EVERYTHING IN & LET IT DO THE WORK)
⑩ WHEN THE PAN IS REALLY HOT
⑪ TAKE IT OFF THE HEAT & BRUSH WITH OIL
⑫ PUT IT BACK ON THE HEAT— WHEN OIL IS HOT
⑯ CHECK THAT IT HAS BY RUNNING A SPATULA AROUND THE EDGE
⑰ NOW TURN IT OVER I FIND THE EASIEST WAY IS TO USE YOUR HANDS
①
②
③
㉑
YOU MIGHT EVEN BE ABLE TO TOSS THEM
㉒ YOU CAN SERVE THEM IMEDIATELY WITH SUGAR & LEMON OR JAM ETC.
JAM
BUT I LIKE MAKING SAVOURY DISHES WITH PANCAKES
SEE FOLLOWING PAGES

MUSHROOM PANCAKES

CANNELONIS

FILLING: BROWN SOME CHOPPED ONIONS PLUS MINCED MEAT ADD SALT & PEPPER & CHOPPED PARSLEY

FILL EACH PANCAKE

ROLL

& PLACE IN BUTTERED OVEN PROOF DISH

POUR OVER:
1) TOMATO SAUCE (PAGE 74)
2) BÉCHAMEL SAUCE (PAGE 78)
3) GRATED CHEESE

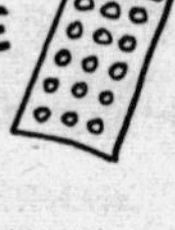

POP INTO A HOT OVEN UNTIL TOP IS DARK GOLD

CAREFUL WHEN YOU EAT THEM THEY'RE VERY HOT

COURGETTE OMELETTE

TRY SPINACH OR LEEKS PRE-COOKED IN THE SAME WAY

THESE OMELETTES COULD ALSO BE COOKED IN A BUTTERED OVEN PROOF DISH FOR ABOUT 45/60 MINUTES IN A SLOW PRE-HEATED OVEN 350°F MARK 3 (KEEP COVERED FOR FIRST HALF HOUR)

MEAT & VEGETABLE OMELETTE

DO STAY FOR A BITE— IT WONT TAKE LONG TO PREPARE...
I'VE GOT SOME COLD MEAT & CHICKEN LEFTOVERS THEY'LL MAKE A NICE MEAT OMELETTE—
MEAT +6 EGGS
THERE'S ABOUT 8OZ OF MEAT HERE
PLUS ABOUT 5 OR 6 SPRING ONIONS
CHOP 3 OR 4 Tomatoes INTO SMALL CUBES
+ THE GREEN PARTS OF THE SPRING ONIONS DISCARD ANY DISCOLOURED BITS & KEEP THE WHITE PARTS FOR SALAD
Mince THE MEAT ADD VEGETABLES + A HANDFUL OF CHOPPED PARSLEY
MIX WELL
ADD THE EGGS ONE AT A TIME STIRRING GENTLY
DO NOT BEAT
ADD SALT, PEPPER SOME FRESH Herbs OR A TEASPOON OF MIXED SPICES
LINE A PRE-HEATED HEAVY PAN WITH OIL AND SPREAD IT ALL OVER
9" PAN
DON'T FORGET THE SIDES...
WHEN REALLY HOT
POUR IN THE MIXTURE COVER. AFTER 10 MINUTES
LOWER HEAT
POP UNDER GRILL
TO SET TOP
EAT WITH SALAD
THERE'S ENOUGH LEFT OVER FOR A COLD LUNCH TOMORROW!

POACHED EGGS IN SWEET CORN

BUTTER +
CORN + CHEESE + EGG

ADD SALT, PEPPER, TOMATO PURÉE (OR HOME-MADE TOMATO SAUCE (PAGE 74))
ADD A LITTLE WATER, LOWER HEAT

SIMMER UNTIL COOKED

(THE TIME WILL VARY WITH TYPE & AGE OF THE VEGETABLES)

SERVE SPRINKLED WITH CHOPPED PARSLEY.

VARIATIONS

1. INSTEAD OF THE TOMATO SPRINKLE A LITTLE TURMERIC POWDER & ADD A SQUEEZE OF LEMON JUICE.

2. NEW POTATOES ARE DELICIOUS COOKED WHOLE IN THEIR JACKETS IN THIS WAY— FLAVOURED WITH SEA SALT & LIME JUICE

3. FOR A SUBSTANTIAL DISH BROWN SOME MEAT CUT UP IN CUBES (LAMB, VEAL OR BEEF) OR SOME FRIED MINCED MEAT BALLS & ADD TO THE VEGETABLES COOK IN THE SAME WAY.

☆ SERVE WITH RICE.

RATATOUILLE

I'VE GOT SOME
RATATOUILLE
LEFT OVER—

BUT IT'S HARDLY
ENOUGH FOR TWO

WELL, I CAN STRETCH IT
WITH 1 BEATEN EGG
& SOME GRATED CHEESE
AND IT WILL MAKE A
DELICIOUS RATATOUILLE
QUICHE!

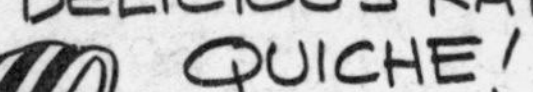

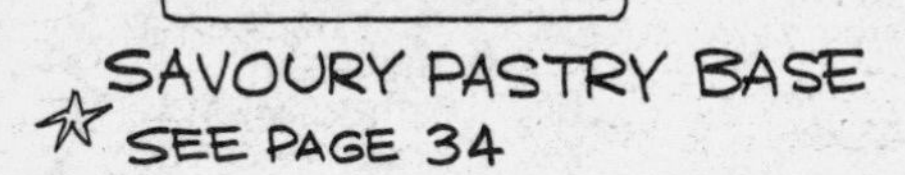

SAVOURY PASTRY BASE
☆ SEE PAGE 34

STUFFED VEGETABLES MAKE A DELICIOUS AND SUBSTANTIAL DISH. I ALWAYS USE MORE OR LESS THE SAME FILLING

- MINCE MEAT
- RICE
- ONIONS

} ALL RAW

THE PROPORTIONS CAN VARY

YOU WILL NEED CHOPPED PARSLEY AND SEASONING

(DILLWEED IS PARTICULARLY APPROPRIATE) SO IS CINNAMON

Cabbage?
THE GREEN ONE, PLEASE I NEED IT FOR STUFFING
NOW...
I'LL JUST BLANCH IT FOR A FEW MINUTES...
BOILING WATER
Meanwhile— the stuffing...
ONE ONION
DO YOU COOK IT FIRST?
NO— EVERYTHING GOES IN RAW!
4oz MINCED MEAT
2oz RICE...
SALT & PEPPER SOME DILL OR CHOPPED PARSLEY
Hmm... THAT'S NICE!
NOW—THE LEAVES ARE SOFT ENOUGH TO HANDLE...
CAREFUL— THEY'RE HOT
Ouch!
IT IS HOT!
A DROP OF OIL TO GREASE THE PAN—
2 OR 3 LEAVES TO LINE IT.
HEAVY PAN
NOW WE STUFF THE OTHER LEAVES ONE BY ONE
stuffing
1 FOLD & ROLL
2 FOLD IN ENDS
3 FINISH WITH A SAUSAGE-LIKE PARCEL
PLACE THEM CAREFULLY INTO THE PAN...
POUR OVER: TWO SPOONFULS OF TOMATO PURÉE IN A GLASS OF WATER...
+ 3 SPOONFULS OF OIL + THE JUICE OF 2 LEMONS...
PUSH
COVER WITH A PLATE—PUSH IT WELL DOWN— THEN COVER WITH A LID & Simmer...
after about 3/4 hour...
YES— IT'S DONE
BUT IT NEEDS MORE LEMON...
CAN BE EATEN HOT OR COLD!
—I PREFER IT COLD!

YOU CAN USE ALL KIND OF VEGETABLES IN THIS WAY...

TRY GREEN PEPPERS

AND ONIONS...

CUT OFF TOP & REMOVE SEEDS

IF SMALL— USE WHOLE IF LARGE— CUT IN HALF

EITHER WAY FOR A NICER FLAVOUR...

FIRST FRY THE PEPPERS IN HOT OIL

COOL ON KITCHEN PAPER TO DRAIN THE OIL

☆ THEN STUFF AND COOK AS STUFFED CABBAGE

ONIONS

1 LARGE ONION

CUT & DISCARD BOTH ENDS & FIRST LAYER OF SKIN

SLIT HALF WAY TO MIDDLE

THEN THROW INTO BOILING WATER

COOK UNTIL LAYERS COME OFF EASILY

SOMETIMES YOU HAVE TO THROW THE INSIDE BACK INTO THE BOILING WATER

WHEN COLD THE LAYERS ARE READY TO STUFF

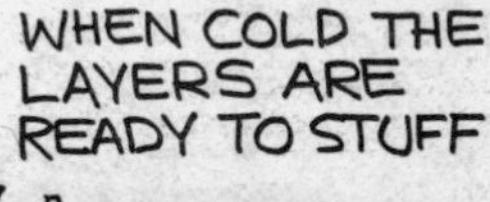

COOK AS FOR CABBAGE

☆ AND A FEW MINUTES BEFORE SERVING PREPARE A CARAMEL MADE OF 3 TABLESPOONS OF SUGAR + ONE OF WATER + A SQUEEZE OF LEMON.

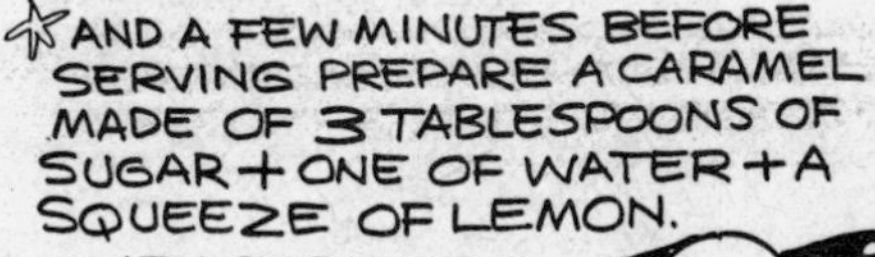

WHEN DARK GOLD POUR OVER ONIONS

STUFFED LEEKS

COURGETTES

☆ I HIT ON THE LEEK RECIPE BY MISTAKE (honest)

IT ACTUALLY DERIVES FROM A SYRIAN DISH MADE WITH STUFFED COURGETTES (YOU CAN TRY THIS TOO)

SCRAPE THEM FIRST

THEN CORE THEM...

WHOLE ONES IF SMALL ENOUGH
IF NOT, CUT THEM IN HALF

CHOP UP THE INSIDE MIX SOME WITH THE STUFFING

STUFF THE COURGETTES AND COOK IN THE SAME WAY

☆ YOU CAN ALSO ADD A TABLESPOON OF TOMATO PUREÉ

ABOUT 6oz STUFFING FOR 1lb COURGETTES SHOULD DO

RICE
PASTA &
SAUCES

RIC
FLO
OIL
Butter

RICE

FOR ME THERE ARE ONLY TWO METHODS

FOR LARGER QUANTITIES I PREFER THE PERSIAN VERSION. PAGE 70

✶ YOU CAN MAKE A PINK
OR YELLOW RICE

BY ADDING A TEASPOONFUL
OF TOMATO PURÉE (PINK)

OR TURMERIC POWDER (YELLOW)
TO THE GLASS OF WATER

✶ IT'S NOT ONLY PRETTIER
BUT THE FLAVOUR IS NICE!

RICE: A PERSIAN METHOD

SOAK THE RICE
(BASMATI IS BEST
A GLASSFUL FOR

3)

FOR A COUPLE OF HOURS

THROW INTO A PAN OF BOILING WATER
(SALTED WATER)

NO NEED TO MEASURE THE WATER HERE—JUST PLENTY OF IT AS FOR COOKING PASTA

STIR, BRING TO THE BOIL AGAIN & SLIGHTLY LOWER HEAT
(WATCH THAT IT DOESN'T BOIL OVER)

AFTER ABOUT 3 OR 4 MINUTES

STRAIN THE RICE

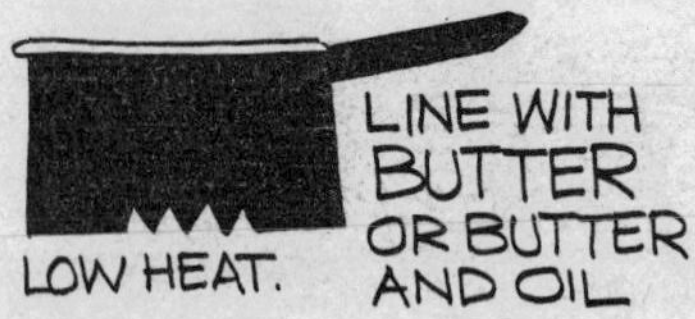

LOW HEAT.

LINE WITH BUTTER OR BUTTER AND OIL

THROW THE RICE BACK INTO PAN

ADD PATS OF BUTTER OVER SURFACE...
COVER THE PAN & PLACE TEA TOWEL UNDER THE LID

LEAVE ON VERY LOW HEAT FOR ANOTHER 20 MINUTES—

MIX WELL BEFORE SERVING

IF YOUR PAN IS VERY HEAVY —— AND YOU LEAVE IT TO COOK ON A VERY VERY LOW HEAT...

YOU WILL GET A LOVELY CRUSTY GOLDEN BASE

IT'S DELICIOUS!

I COULD LIVE ON PASTA
LARGE OR SMALL, THIN
OR THICK, BAKED OR

* SERVED JUST WITH BUTTER
OR GRATED PARMESAN
* OR WITH THE JUICES OF
A POT ROAST OR
CASSEROLE
* OR A WELL FLAVOURED
TOMATO SAUCE
* OR A BOLOGNAISE SAUCE
* A PESTO SAUCE OR A
CARBONARA SAUCE

BOLOGNAISE SAUCE

A HEAVY PAN

SOFTEN & REALLY BROWN A CHOPPED MEDIUM ONION

THEN ADD: CHOPPED CLOVE OF GARLIC AND ONE LARGE GRATED CARROT

THEN ADD ABOUT HALF A POUND OF LEAN MINCED MEAT

WHEN REALLY **BROWN** ADD SMALL TIN OF TOMATO PURÉE

SALT & PEPPER

THYME & A BAY LEAF

A LITTLE BIT OF WATER & SIMMER

IT SHOULD BE READY IN ABOUT ½ HOUR BUT I LIKE TO REDUCE IT AS MUCH AS POSSIBLE WITHOUT BURNING OF COURSE.

CARBONARA

SAUTÉ BITS OF BACON

WHEN ALL THE FAT HAS MELTED ADD: BEATEN EGG & PARMESAN CHEESE

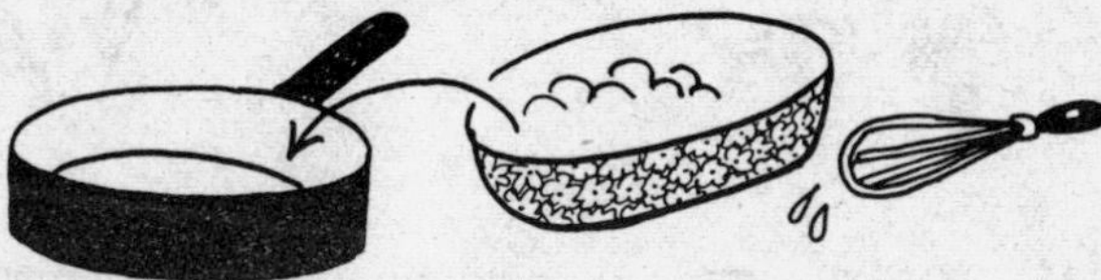

GIVE IT A STIR & POUR INTO THE DRAINED PASTA

TOMATO SAUCE...

①

②

FIRST SOFTEN THE CHOPPED ONIONS IN OIL (OR OIL + BUTTER)

⑥

WHEN THE ONIONS TURN **GOLD**

ADD SOME CHOPPED GARLIC

⑦

WHEN THEY START BROWNING ADD THE TOMATOES

PLUS A SMALL TIN OF TOMATO PURÉE

⑪

IT SHOULD BE READY TO USE AFTER ABOUT **20** MINUTES

⑫

BUT TASTE TO MAKE SURE & ADJUST SEASONING

☆IF YOU LIKE A HOT SAUCE OR IF THE RECIPE REQUIRES ONE, THIS IS WHEN YOU ADD A CHILLI...

BASIC STEP BY STEP RECIPE

PESTO SAUCE À LA SUZY

PESTO SAUCE

NOW LET'S TRY THE REAL ONE

POUND 2 CLOVES OF GARLIC

THEN ADD: CHOPPED SWEET BASIL LEAVES (APPROX 2 OZ)

+ ABOUT 2oz GRATED PARMESAN

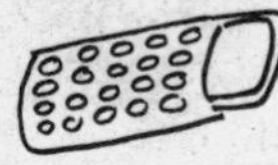

AND – IF YOU'VE GOT THEM, ABOUT 2oz PINE NUTS

POUND WELL & ADD OIL GRADUALLY LIKE A MAYONNAISE (ABOUT 3 TABLESPOONS)

OR BLEND THE WHOLE LOT TOGETHER IN AN ELECTRIC BLENDER

ADD SALT & PEPPER

STIR INTO SPAGHETTI

✶ QUANTITY FOR ABOUT 1lb SPAGHETTI

BÉCHAMEL SAUCE

* FOR A LEMON SAUCE MAKE IT WITH CHICKEN

BASIC STEP BY STEP RECIPE...

③ YOU SPRINKLE & STIR THE FLOUR INTO THE BUTTER

④ TAKE PAN OFF THE HEAT —— & START ADDING LIQUIDS (MILK, STOCK OR BROTH)

YOU WILL NEED ROUGHLY 1½ PINTS

⑦ A LITTLE MORE LIQUID

⑧ STIR VIGOROUSLY WHEN WELL AMALGAMATED PUT BACK ON **LOW** HEAT STIRRING ALL THE TIME

⑨ REPEAT SEVERAL TIMES UNTIL ALL LIQUID IS ABSORBED.

⑫ HOWEVER, IF THE SAUCE IS TOO LIQUID FOR YOUR PURPOSE YOU CAN NOW INCREASE THE HEAT TO THICKEN IT... STIRRING ALL THE TIME

⑬ NOW IT'S TIME TO SEASON WITH SALT & CHEESE*

& YOU CAN ALSO BEAT IN A COUPLE OF EGGS (LET IT COOL A BIT FIRST)

OR VEAL STOCK & FLAVOUR WITH LEMON JUICE INSTEAD OF CHEESE

BAKED MACARONI

* IT MAKES **8** HEFTY PORTIONS

I ALWAYS HOPE THERE'S SOME LEFT OVER AS I MUST CONFESS I LOVE TO EAT IT COLD NEXT DAY.

FISH FLESH & FOWL

EGYPTIAN FISH FINGERS

* IF YOU'RE USED TO BUYING FROZEN FISH BALLS FROM THE SUPERMARKET — WHY DON'T YOU TRY COOKING THEM LIKE THAT FOR A CHANGE...

BAKED FISH

I'D LIKE A NICE FISH FOR BAKING PLEASE....
JUST THE THING— HERE'S A LOVELY GREY MULLET. 1lb.. FOR 4 PEOPLE—? THEN YOU'D BETTER HAVE TWO
HE'S GUTTED THE FISH—BUT HE ALWAYS SEEMS TO LEAVE SOME SCALES ON—
SCRAPE
SCRAPE
Marinade
SALT & PEPPER.
Juice of 2 Lemons
1 ONION
2 CLOVES OF GARLIC
GRATED
1 GREEN PEPPER CUT INTO FINE STRIPS
CHOPPED PARSLEY
I GRATE THE ONION STRAIGHT INTO THE BOWL SO AS NOT TO WASTE THE JUICE
THIS IS THE EASIEST WAY I KNOW OF CHOPPING PARSLEY-(IT ALSO SAVES FINGERS)
CUT CUT
CUT CUT
MIX ALL THE INGREDIENTS IN THE BOWL
THEN ADD THREE TABLESPOONS OF OIL
STIR & POUR OVER MARINADE THEN LEAVE FOR A COUPLE OF HOURS
*3 SLITS
PRE-HEATED OVEN AT 350° OR GAS MARK 4
THIS SHOULD TAKE 20 TO 25 MINUTES
CAN I USE WINE?
IF YOU LIKE A GLASS OF DRY White Wine POURED OVER THE FISH TEN MINUTES BEFORE SERVING...
SERVE WITH Boiled Potatoes TOSSED IN THE MARINADE (TASTE & ADJUST SEASONING)
P.S. IT'S ALSO DELICIOUS COLD WITH MAYONNAISE

IT'S BETTER IF YOUR BAKING DISH IS LARGE ENOUGH TO HAVE ONE LARGE FISH RATHER THAN TWO SMALLER ONES

(THERE'S LESS WASTE)

YOU CAN ALSO GRILL THE FISH HAVING MARINADED IT IN THE SAME WAY

FISH IN TOMATO SAUCE

A DIFFERENT SAUCE

WHEN THE FISH HAS BEEN FRIED AND TRANSFERRED TO KITCHEN PAPER...

FRY IN THE SAME PAN
4 OR 5 CHOPPED CLOVES OF GARLIC
A WHOLE BUNCH OF CHOPPED PARSLEY

THEN ADD ☆

A SMALL TIN OF TOMATO PURÉE
A CUP OF VINEGAR
A CUP OF WATER

RETURN THE FISH TO THE PAN
COVER & SIMMER UNTIL THE SAUCE THICKENS...

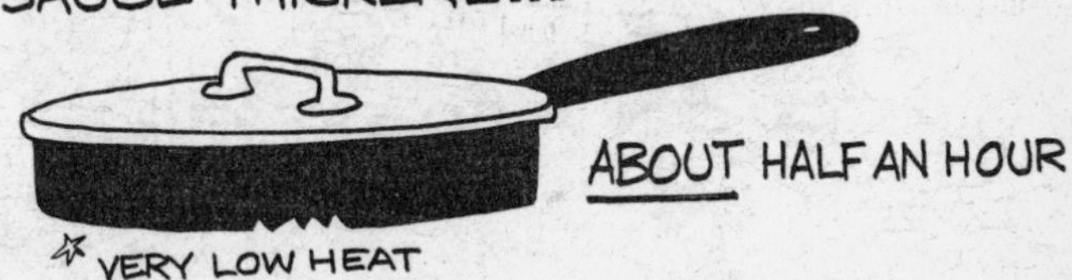

<u>ABOUT</u> HALF AN HOUR

☆ VERY LOW HEAT

ESCOVITCH FISH (FRIED FISH IN HOT SAUCE)

☆ THIS IS A LOVELY JAMAICAN RECIPE WHICH YOU CAN USE WITH SMALL WHOLE FISH (SARDINE OR RED MULLET) OR LARGE SLICED FIRM FLESHED FISH LIKE SNAPPER, BASS, SEA BREAM, JOHN DORY...

YOU CAN ALSO EAT IT COLD

NOW—
I'M FRYING FISH TONIGHT—
SO I'LL MAKE SOME HOT SAUCE TO GO WITH IT...
2 ONIONS
Lightly Fry
THE ONIONS & ADD:
3 or 4 STICKS OF Celery...
AND 1 GREEN PEPPER
ALL CUT INTO STRIPS
ONE small Chilli
REMOVE THE SEEDS
THEY'RE HOT
THEN CUT INTO PIECES
ADD 1 GLASS OF Vinegar
+ ONE TEASPOON OF WHOLE ALLSPICE
Cover & Simmer
IT WILL BE DONE BY THE TIME I FRY THE FISH
ONCE the FISH IS FRIED—ARRANGE ON A PLATTER...
POUR THE SAUCE over
OH BOY OH BOY OH BOY! IT'S HOT
I KNOW THAT HE LIKES HIS FOOD HOT —
YOU CAN OF COURSE MAKE IT WITHOUT THE CHILLI
But the ALLSPICE is a must
MOST SUPERMARKETS WILL HAVE IT

LEG OF LAMB

CHOP INTO SLIVERS 2 OR 3 CLOVES OF GARLIC. INSERT INTO SLITS IN THE FLESHY PART OF THE MEAT
OIL
PUSH SOME GROUND CORIANDER IN AS WELL...
NOW, RUB IT ALL OVER WITH OIL...
LOVELY—NOW SALT, PEPPER AND CORIANDER!
POP IT INTO THE OVEN AT 400 (THAT'S GAS MARK 6)
about 2lbs OF POTATOES
2 LARGE ONIONS
1 LARGE TIN OF PEELED TOMATOES
meanwhile
NOW WE CUT THIS LOT INTO CHUNKS
PUT YOUR VEGETABLES IN AROUND THE MEAT—MIX THEM WELL SO THAT THEY GET COVERED IN OIL & MEAT FAT
*2 BAY LEAVES & A SPRINKLE OF THYME
AFTER ABOUT 1 hour...
—I'LL TAKE IT OUT AND TURN THE MEAT OVER AND MIX THE VEGETABLES
GENTLY NOW—THAT FAT IS HOT
POP IT BACK FOR ANOTHER COUPLE OF HOURS IN A SLOW OVEN (300° GAS MARK 2) OR UNTIL Tender
THE VEGETABLES ARE ALWAYS A BIT MUSHY—BUT WHO CARES—?
OH BOY
NOT ME—NOT WHEN THEY SMELL AND TASTE LIKE THAT!

VARIATION

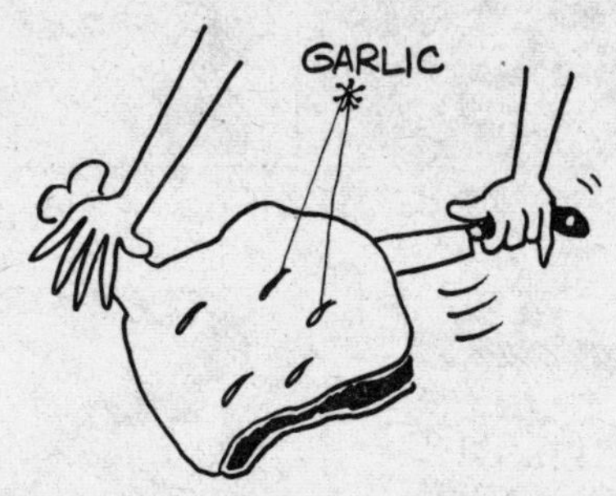

THIS IS ALSO VERY NICE WITH A SHOULDER — BUT I LIKE TO TRIM OFF AS MUCH OF THE FAT AS POSSIBLE

RUB WITH SALT & PEPPER & CORIANDER

☆ INSTEAD OF THE VEGETABLES TRY THIS WITH ANY SMALL TYPE PASTA. COOK IN BOILING WATER STRAIN & THROW IN PAN WITH THE MEAT — MIX WELL

PORK WITH APRICOTS & PRUNES

☆ THE FRUIT ENRICHES THE RATHER DRY PORK MEAT...

AND IT WORKS EVEN BETTER WITH LAMB!

OSSO BUCCO (KNUCKLE OF VEAL)

* THIS CUT IS CONSIDERED A DELICACY IN ITALY & FRANCE,

  BUT IS QUITE NEGLECTED IN BRITAIN...

* BUTCHERS USUALLY CUT UP THE MEAT & MIX IT WITH OTHER BITS & PIECES TO SELL AS VEAL PIE, THEREFORE THE PRICE WILL VARY ACCORDING TO THE AREA YOU LIVE IN...

* A BUTCHER WHO HAS MANY FRENCH & ITALIAN CUSTOMERS WILL KNOW EXACTLY HOW TO CUT IT —BUT HE WILL CHARGE MORE

I THINK I'LL MAKE SOME OSSO-BUCCO TONIGHT—I'VE GOT ENOUGH WINE!
DRY White Wine
SHOPPING LIST
1 TIN OF ANCHOVY FILLETS
1 TIN TOMATO PURÉE
GARLIC
LIME OR LEMON & PARSLEY
SEE BUTCHER
LISTEN LADY—I KNOW WHAT OSSO BUCCO IS—A KNUCKLE OF VEAL SAWN INTO SLICES—RIGHT?
BLOOMIN' CHEEK!
YES—BUT ONLY THE MIDDLE PIECES PLEASE—WHERE THE BONE IS TINY, YOU MAY HAVE TO CUT 2 KNUCKLES
YES—THAT'S FINE!
NOW, JUST ROLL THE MEAT IN THE FLOUR
FLOUR
I LIKE A MIXTURE OF BUTTER & OIL TO SAUTÉ THE MEAT—ABOUT 2 SPOONFULS OF OIL AND 2 oz OF BUTTER
BUTTER
OIL
NOW THAT THE MEAT HAS A NICE GOLDEN COLOUR, I'LL ADD A GLASSFUL OF WHITE WINE — SCRAPE THE PAN, BRING TO THE BOIL, SALT TO TASTE, NOW COVER AND LET IT SIMMER....
Cheers GIRLS!
1½ hrs LATER... THE MEAT IS NICE & TENDER, I CAN PREPARE THE SAUCE NOW...
CHOP & THROW INTO THE POT 3 LARGE CLOVES OF GARLIC. 5 ANCHOVY FILLETS, A HANDFUL OF PARSLEY—STRIPS OF LEMON PEEL 1 TIN OF TOMATO PURÉE...
STIR AND LET IT SIMMER FOR ANOTHER HOUR
WHAT ABOUT THE WATER?
BUT IF IT'S BEEN ABSORBED ADD ONE CUP OF WATER
WELL, THERE WAS THE WINE—AND I'VE SALTED THE MEAT. THIS SHOULD RELEASE ENOUGH JUICES FOR THE MEAT TO COOK—
YOU GET A LOVELY THICK SAUCE WITHOUT ARTIFICIAL THICKENING — SERVE ON A BED OF RICE...
Mmm Just smell that....!

VEAL STEW & PEAS

* THIS IS A FRENCH VERSION OF OSSO BUCCO —

YOU CAN HAVE IT CUT AS IN THE PREVIOUS RECIPE OR YOU CAN JUST USE THE MEAT

A CHOPPED UP BONE WILL MAKE A GOOD VEAL STOCK — OR YOUR PET DOG VERY HAPPY

I'D LIKE 1lb OF Veal FOR STEWING PLEASE BUTCHER
PREFERABLY FROM THE KNUCKLE
YOU'RE LUCKY— I HAVEN'T CUT IT ALL UP FOR THE WEEKEND YET!
(IT USUALLY GOES INTO THE PIE VEAL DISH)
SAUTÉ 3 MEDIUM ONIONS CUT INTO CHUNKS.
OIL & BUTTER
CUT THE MEAT INTO CHUNKS & ROLL IN FLOUR
THE ONIONS ARE SOFT... NOW I'LL ADD THE MEAT
STIR UNTIL NICE AND BROWN
NOW ADD WATER TO COVER
COVER
SALT & PEPPER BRING TO THE BOIL
LOWER HEAT COVER & SIMMER
AFTER ABOUT 1½ hrs
IT'S DONE— BUT NOT SOFT ENOUGH
YOU SHOULD BE ABLE TO CUT IT WITH A FORK
THEN ADD:
1lb FROZEN Peas
PEAS
BETTER STILL— 1lb OF FRESH ONES!
THEY SHOULD TAKE ABOUT 45 MINS TO COOK AND ABSORB ALL THAT LOVELY FLAVOUR---
SERVE WITH POTATOES OR RICE

ROAST VEAL KNUCKLE

SHIN OR LEG — OF BEEF & VEAL KNUCKLE ARE MY FAVOURITE CUTS FOR SLOW COOKING DISHES & THEY ARE USUALLY MUCH CHEAPER THAN OTHER CUTS

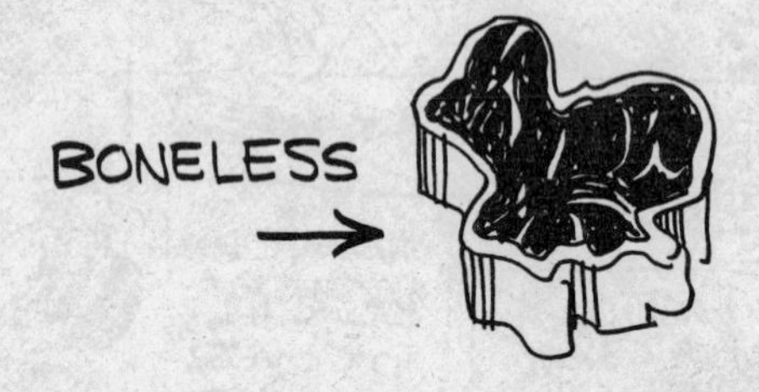

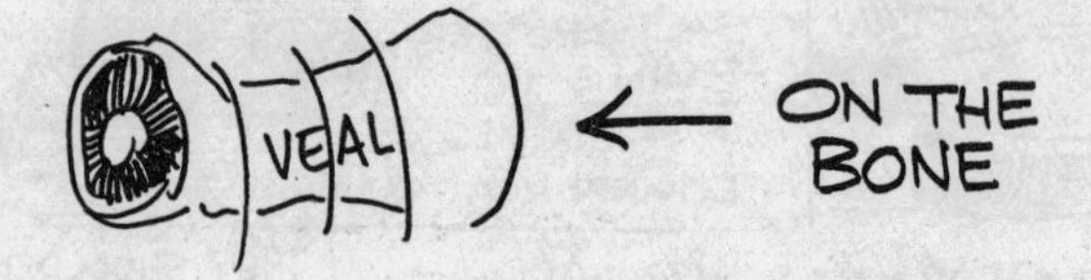

* THE MEAT SHOULD ALWAYS BE COOKED SO TENDER THAT YOU COULD CUT IT WITH A FORK

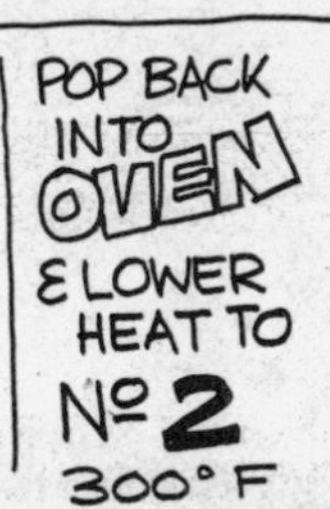

FOR THE LAST
½ hour —
YOU COULD DROP
INTO THE PAN
SOME
NEW
POTATOES

SHIN OF BEEF WITH PASTA

☆ TRY COOKING THE SAME MEAT WITH POTATOES INSTEAD OF PASTA

WHEN THE MEAT GETS TO THE SIMMERING STAGE

SPRINKLE A TABLESPOON OF TURMERIC POWDER & SQUEEZE THE JUICE OF A LEMON OR LIME

WASH & PEEL THE POTATOES
CUT THEM INTO CHUNKS
BRIEFLY DEEP FRY IN OIL UNTIL GOLDEN BUT NOT WHOLLY COOKED

MOUSSAKA

3 LARGE Aubergines
SLICED
SPRINKLE WITH SALT.
WEIGHT IT DOWN
AND LEAVE IT FOR A FEW HOURS UNTIL ALL THE BITTER JUICES HAVE RUN OUT....
Pat dry
AND THEN
FRY
IN HOT OIL
WHEN GOLDEN, DRAIN ON KITCHEN PAPER
THEN FRY 1lb OF CHOPPED ONIONS
YOU MAY HAVE TO ADD MORE OIL
WHEN ONIONS ARE BROWN
ADD 1lb OF MINCED MEAT
BROWN THE LOT, AND ADD:
Salt, Pepper, thyme...
→ TO TASTE ←
ONE BAYLEAF +
ONE TABLESPOON
Tomato Purée
A LITTLE Water
...AND SCRAPE THE PAN...
COVER & SIMMER...
Meanwhile:
THE WHITE SAUCE
Melt 2oz. BUTTER
MEDIUM LOW HEAT
LIFT OFF HEAT
AND STIR IN ONE HEAPED TABLESPOON OF FLOUR
AND ADD A LITTLE MILK
BACK ON HEAT, THEN
LIFT AGAIN
ADD MORE MILK,
STIR
BACK ON HEAT
REPEAT THIS UNTIL YOU'VE USED 1 PINT OF MILK
ADD: SALT & GRATED CHEESE (ABOUT 2oz)
LET SAUCE THICKEN ON VERY LOW HEAT
AND STIR...
*
ALL THIS MUST BE DONE THOROUGHLY & SLOWLY TO AVOID LUMPS & THAT HORRIBLE FLOUR TASTE
UGH!
BEAT (VIGOROUSLY)
ONE LARGE EGG INTO SAUCE
THEN POUR OVER THE PREPARED OVEN PROOF DISH
LAYERS OF:
AUBERGINES
MEAT
AUBERGINES
MEAT
AUBERGINES
THEN 1 HOUR IN OVEN GAS MARK 4. 350° DEG.F

✩ TRY USING TURNIPS INSTEAD OF AUBERGINES!

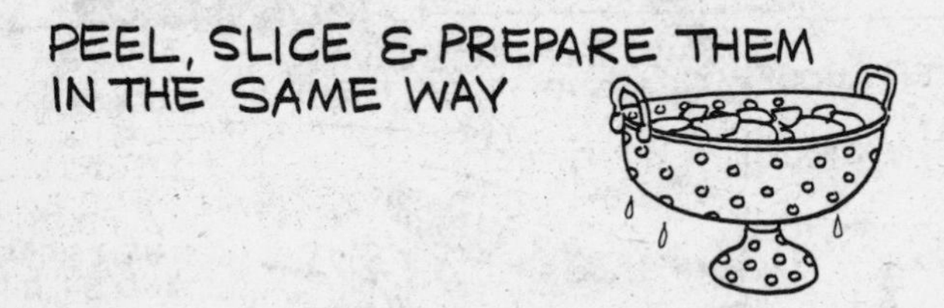

PEEL, SLICE & PREPARE THEM IN THE SAME WAY

✩ I BET VERY FEW PEOPLE WILL GUESS WHAT YOU'VE DONE

(OK IF YOU'RE A PURIST— DON'T CALL IT MOUSSAKA BUT YOU WILL ENJOY IT JUST AS MUCH)

BROAD BEANS & MINCE

A SPRINKLE OF CHOPPED PARSLEY OR FRESH CORIANDER GIVES THIS DISH EXTRA FLAVOUR AND COLOUR

MEATBALLS

1lb MINCED BEEF
OR Beef & Lamb mixed...
One egg
Piece of STALE BREAD IN MILK
MEATBALLS IN TOMATO SAUCE & RICE TONIGHT
ONE ONION
CHOPPED PARSLEY
FIRST SALT & PEPPER - THEN ONION & CHOPPED PARSLEY
* AND I LIKE A PINCH OF CUMIN POWDER!
AMALGAMATE WELL - UGH!
SQUELCH
* USE GLOVES IF YOU MUST!
THERE'S PLENTY FOR 4 SO I'VE PINCHED SOME FOR MY LUNCH!
ONE HAMBURGER
ADD THE EGG TO BIND MIXTURE...
AND THE BREAD TO MAKE IT SOFT & LIGHT
PHEW!
MIX ONCE AGAIN!
MAKE WALNUT SIZE MEATBALLS!
ROLL ROLL
ROLL ROLL
ROLL IN BREADCRUMBS
A LITTLE OIL
FRY GENTLY
KITCHEN PAPER
WHEN GOLDEN LIFT & PUT ASIDE
ALL THE MEAT IS DONE - NOW THE SAUCE
FRY A CHOPPED ONION, A CLOVE OF GARLIC THEN ADD THE TOMATO PURÉE
SMALL TIN
ONE GLASS OF Water OR Stock
AND - BACK GO THE MEATBALLS!
OOPS! - A LITTLE MORE SALT!
COVER & Simmer ON A LOW HEAT - IT WILL BE COOKED IN 15 MINUTES...
* I'LL RE-HEAT IT TONIGHT!

* I USALLY LIKE MAKING MEATBALLS WITH RAW MINCED MEAT —

BUT COOKED BEEF OR LAMB LEFTOVERS CAN BE PREPARED IN THE SAME WAY TO EAT WITH RICE OR BREAD

* THE MEAT CAN ALSO BE MIXED WITH LEFT OVER (OR FRESH & LIGHTLY SAUTÉD) VEGETABLES SUCH AS LEEKS SPINACH POTATOES ETC.

* TRY USING — INSTEAD OF TOMATO PURÉE A TEASPOONFUL  OF TURMERIC & LEMON JUICE

KOFTA (BARBECUE MINCE)

THESE CAN BE
GRILLED INDOORS...

YOU CAN ALSO ALTER
THE SHAPE:

TAKE A WALNUT SIZE
LUMP OF MEAT...

& JUST FLATTEN
IT SLIGHTLY →

EAT WITH EGYPTIAN SALAD
(PAGE 27) & FRESH BREAD

* OR INCLUDE IN THE INDIAN MEAL
LISTED ON PAGE 135

CHILLI CON CARNE

THEY'RE DRIVING ME MAD—I'M NOT SURE HOW MANY WILL BE COMING TO DINNER TOMORROW NIGHT... SIX... EIGHT OR TEN?

OH—I DON'T SEE WHY YOU WORRY SO, SUZY—MAKE YOUR CHILLI CON CARNE EVERYBODY LOVES IT YOU DON'T NEED TO COOK AN EXACT AMOUNT AND LEFT OVERS CAN GO INTO THE FRIDGE OR FREEZER...

AND I WOULDN'T MIND MAKING ANOTHER MEAL OF IT

YOU'RE RIGHT
I CAN ALSO
MAKE IT IN
STAGES—
TONIGHT I'LL
SOAK THE
BEANS

1lb OF DRIED
RED BEANS
(OR KIDNEY BEANS)

& TOMORROW
MORNING I'LL
GET ON WITH THE
COOKING
OF THE
BEANS

SAUTÉ IN OIL
1 LARGE CHOPPED
ONION + 3 CLOVES
OF GARLIC

WHEN GOLDEN
SPRINKLE WITH A
TABLESPOON OF
CUMIN POWDER
STIR WELL
DON'T LET IT BURN

NOW ADD:
THE BEANS WITH
WATER TO COVER

BRING TO
THE BOIL

LOWER HEAT, HALF
COVER & SIMMER
UNTIL TENDER

NOW, SAUTÉ
1lb MINCED
MEAT
ADD 1 GRATED
ONION
WHEN BROWN
ADD 1 SMALL
TIN TOMATO
PURÉE

+1 CHILLI
(REMOVE SEEDS)

NOW TRANSFER
TO THE BEAN
PAN & ADD SALT
& PEPPER

TASTE &
ADJUST..
LOW HEAT

☆ NOW I CAN PUT
MY FEET UP FOR
A WHILE BEFORE
I GET DRESSED IT
WILL BE READY
TO EAT IN ABOUT
AN HOUR—

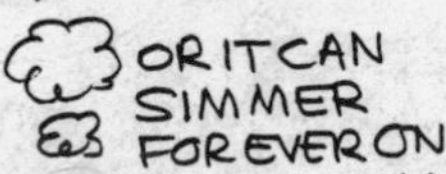

OR IT CAN
SIMMER
FOREVER ON
A VERY SLOW HEAT

IT'S VERY
USEFUL WHEN
YOU HAVE
UN-PUNCTUAL
GUESTS

☆ I LIKE TO SERVE IT WITH RICE & EGYPTIAN SALAD
(SEE PAGE 27)

MEAT CURRY

I FIRST QUICKLY FRY THE MEAT IN 1/2 CARTON OF YOGURT
YOG
Meat (about 1lb) OF Lamb or Beef cut into cubes
THE YOGURT IS ALL DRIED UP NOW— I'LL ADD THE REST OF THE CARTON
AND Stir...
ADD:
Your favourite curry Powder TO suit your own taste
I PREFER MY OWN MIXTURE
WHICH I OFTEN VARY FOR EXAMPLE:
1/2 teaspoon of TURMERIC
1/4 OF CUMIN
1/2 OF CORIANDER
ALL IN POWDER FORM.
4 OR 5 CARDAMOM PODS.
A FEW CLOVES & A PINCH OF CAYENNE PEPPER.
ALSO ADD: 1 Large GRATED ONION
STIR ON HIGH FLAME UNTIL BROWN.
NOW ADD 1 GLASS OF WATER salt..
COVER AND LOWER HEAT
Simmer UNTIL Tender
THE GRATED ONION MAKES A THICK RICH SAUCE
10 OR 15 MINUTES BEFORE SERVING THROW IN:
1 PACKET OF FROZEN PEAS
THE PEAS WILL ABSORB ALL THAT LOVELY FLAVOUR!
EAT WITH RICE AND VARIOUS GARNISHES
CURRY
RICE
CHUTNEY
ONIONS
MARINADED
CUCUMBER
PICKLED LIMES

IF YOU LIKE — INSTEAD OF YOGURT YOU CAN BROWN THE MEAT IN A VERY HOT OIL AND BUTTER MIXTURE

AND OF COURSE — YOU NEED **NOT** ADD THE PEAS!

* THIS DISH CAN BE INCLUDED IN THE INDIAN MENU LISTED ON PAGE 135

OX TONGUE

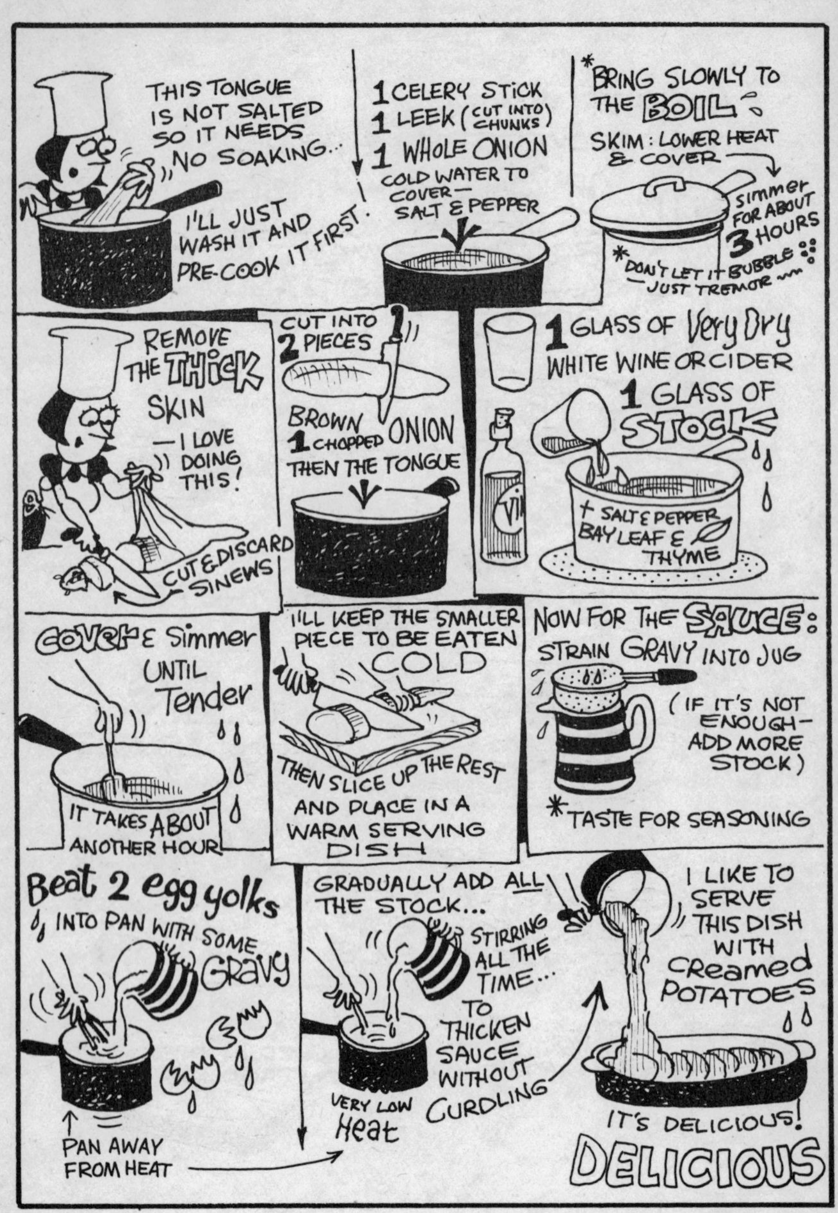

THIS TONGUE IS NOT SALTED SO IT NEEDS NO SOAKING...
I'LL JUST WASH IT AND PRE-COOK IT FIRST.
1 CELERY STICK
1 LEEK (CUT INTO CHUNKS)
1 WHOLE ONION
COLD WATER TO COVER—
SALT & PEPPER
*BRING SLOWLY TO THE BOIL
SKIM: LOWER HEAT & COVER
SIMMER FOR ABOUT 3 HOURS
*DON'T LET IT BUBBLE — JUST TREMOR
REMOVE THE THICK SKIN
— I LOVE DOING THIS!
CUT & DISCARD SINEWS
CUT INTO 2 PIECES
BROWN 1 CHOPPED ONION THEN THE TONGUE
1 GLASS OF Very Dry WHITE WINE OR CIDER
1 GLASS OF STOCK
+ SALT & PEPPER BAY LEAF & THYME
VIN
COVER & Simmer UNTIL Tender
IT TAKES ABOUT ANOTHER HOUR
I'LL KEEP THE SMALLER PIECE TO BE EATEN COLD
THEN SLICE UP THE REST AND PLACE IN A WARM SERVING DISH
NOW FOR THE SAUCE:
STRAIN GRAVY INTO JUG
(IF IT'S NOT ENOUGH- ADD MORE STOCK)
*TASTE FOR SEASONING
Beat 2 egg yolks INTO PAN WITH SOME GRAVY
PAN AWAY FROM HEAT
GRADUALLY ADD ALL THE STOCK...
STIRRING ALL THE TIME...
TO THICKEN SAUCE WITHOUT CURDLING
VERY LOW Heat
I LIKE TO SERVE THIS DISH WITH Creamed POTATOES
IT'S DELICIOUS!
DELICIOUS

ANOTHER WAY:
WHEN COOKED THICK & TENDER

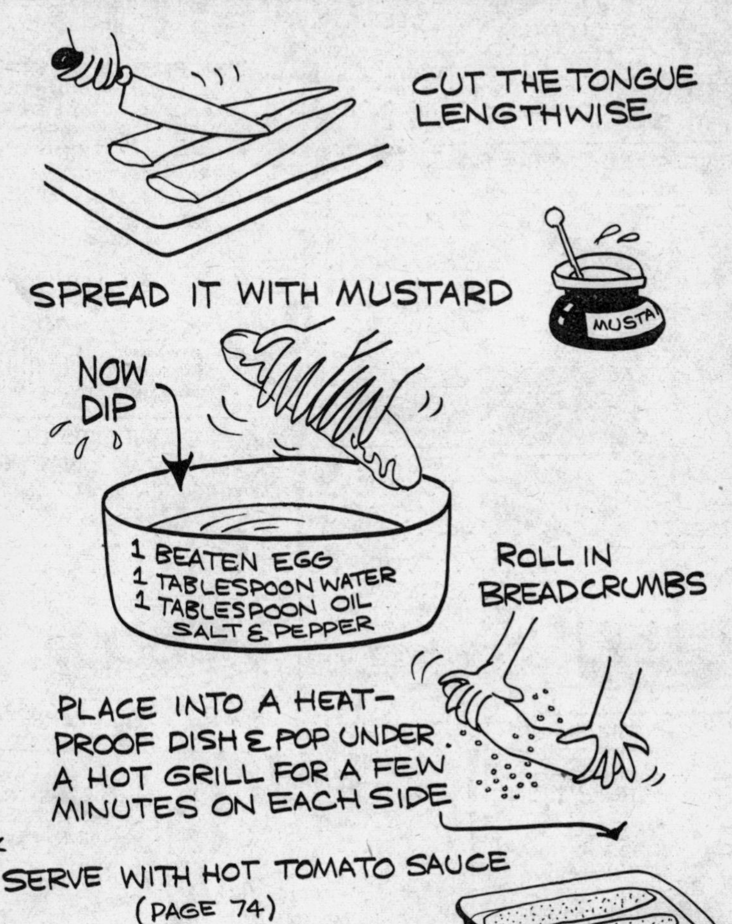

PIG'S TROTTERS & HARICOT BEANS

WELL—IT'S EVEN NICER
WITH CALVES' FEET...

WASH & PREPARE THE STOCK
IN THE SAME WAY, —
BUT WHEN YOU'VE STRAINED IT
REMOVE ALL THE BONES

THEN PROCEED IN THE SAME WAY...

LAMBS' HEARTS

BRAISED CALVES' HEARTS

JUST CUT THEM IN HALF & WASH & REMOVE ARTERIES

SAUTÉ IN BUTTER/OIL MIXTURE WITH A FEW SMALL WHOLE ONIONS

WHEN BROWN ADD A GLASS OF WATER OR STOCK & SALT & PEPPER

ADD 1lb OF SLICED CARROTS COVER & LOWER HEAT

SIMMER FOR ABOUT 1 HOUR

INCREASE THE HEAT, REDUCE TO THICK SAUCE CONSISTENCY & POUR OVER THE DISH

CHICKEN LIVER & VERMICELLI

CALVES' LIVER À LA LYONNAISE

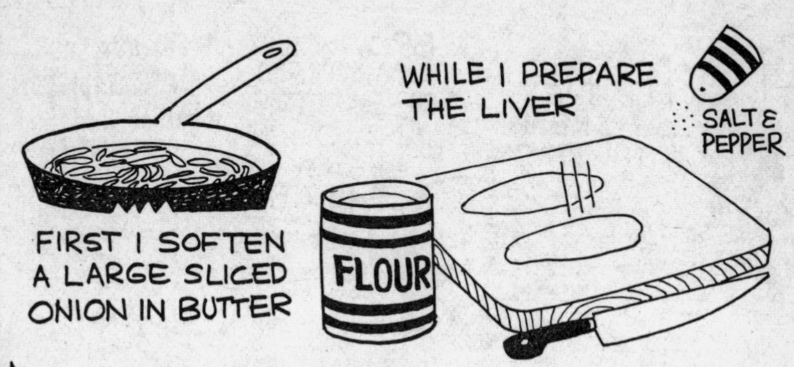

NOW THE ONIONS ARE A LOVELY GOLDEN COLOUR

THEN FRY
THE LIVER IN THE SAME PAN
A COUPLE OF MINUTES ON EACH SIDE
& TRANSFER ONTO THE SERVING DISH
WITH THE ONIONS.

ADD 1 TABLESPOON OF VINEGAR
TO THE FRYING PAN, INCREASE
HEAT— SCRAPE ALL THE BITS...
THEN POUR OVER THE LIVER.

POT ROAST CHICKEN

WHEN THE FAT IS MELTED
I ADD A LITTLE OIL

IF FOR SOME REASON OR OTHER
THE SAUCE NEEDS THICKENING
DO IT WITH AN EGG YOLK

TAKE THE PAN OFF THE HEAT
TO AVOID CURDLING
POUR THE MIXTURE IN
AND WHISK OFF THE HEAT

*DON'T FORGET TO
REMOVE THE CHICKEN FIRST

GRILLED POUSSIN OR SMALL CHICKEN

☆ USING THE MARINADE AS A BASTE

CHICKEN BREAST À LA THAI

THE CHICKEN WE HAD AT THAT RESTAURANT THE OTHER DAY WAS DELICIOUS
THIS BOOK ON S. ASIAN FOOD GIVES ME SOME VERY GOOD IDEAS

MARINADE SOME BONED CHICKEN BREASTS IN
LIME OR LEMON JUICE
SLIVER OF GARLIC
SMALL GLASS OF DRY SHERRY
ONE CUT UP DRIED RED CHILLI
(DISCARD SEEDS)
OR A PINCH OF CHILLI POWDER
ONE TEASPOON OF BROWN SUGAR
2 OR 3 STRIPS OF GREEN GINGER

* TO COOK

DRY THE CHICKEN PIECES & DIP INTO FLOUR BEFORE FRYING IN A LITTLE OIL

THEN POUR THE MARINADE OVER IT

* IF TOO DRY—ADD A LITTLE WATER

BRING TO THE BOIL
LOWER HEAT
& SIMMER

* IT SHOULDN'T TAKE MORE THAN 15 TO 20 MINUTES

EAT WITH RICE

CHICKEN WINGS

CHICKEN WINGS CAN BE USED TO ENRICH VEGETABLE DISHES

OR IN THEIR OWN RIGHT →

I LOVE CHICKEN WINGS
AND I'M GLAD WE CAN GET WHOLE PACKETS OF THEM
(AND THEY MAKE A LOVELY CHEAP DISH)
FIRST COOK SOME
ONION
IN OIL SLOWLY TO SOFTEN
MEDIUM HEAT
WHEN GOLDEN-
ADD THE WINGS...
BROWN THEM
ADD A LITTLE
WATER
SALT & PEPPER
COVER
& LET IT COOK SLOWLY UNTIL STICKY
—ADD JUST A LITTLE WATER TO SCRAPE THE PAN
SCRAPE SCRAPE
AND YOU GET A THICK SAUCE
THESE CAN BE SERVED WITH
RICE · PASTA
POTATOES
SALAD
BREAD
—AND THE SAUCE!
mmm
I NEVER THOUGHT THAT CHICKEN WINGS COULD BE SO DELICIOUS!

CHICKEN WITH MACARONI

CHICKEN & WHITE LEMON SAUCE

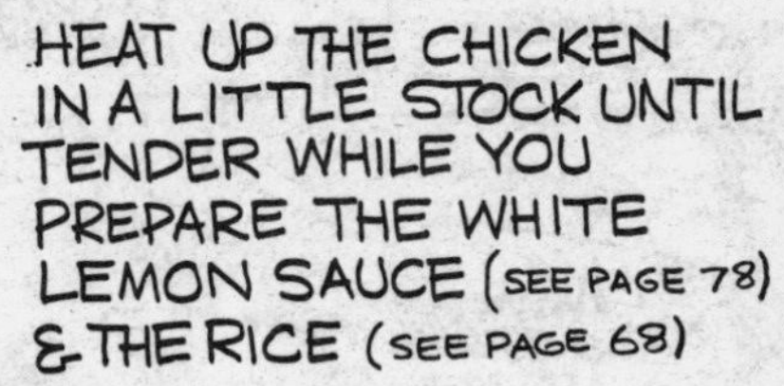

HEAT UP THE CHICKEN IN A LITTLE STOCK UNTIL TENDER WHILE YOU PREPARE THE WHITE LEMON SAUCE (SEE PAGE 78) & THE RICE (SEE PAGE 68)

*TO SERVE

PLACE CHICKEN PIECES ON A DISH OF RICE & POUR LEMON SAUCE OVER

TURMERIC & LEMON CHICKEN

DEEP FRY IN VERY HOT OIL . . .
REMOVE AS SOON AS GOLDEN

☆ THEN ALTHOUGH NOT QUITE
COOKED ADD THEM TO THE
CHICKEN CASSEROLE AND
SIMMER UNTIL THEY'RE DONE

TEST WITH A FORK

TANDOORI CHICKEN

"NOW THAT WE HAVE SUCCEEDED IN THIS EXPERIMENT — WE'LL TRY OUT A WHOLE

INDIAN MEAL

TURKEY OR CHICKEN & CELERY

☆ THIS IS A DELICIOUS WAY OF USING THOSE ENDLESS TURKEY LEFTOVERS —

(YOU CAN USE CHICKEN TOO)

WHAT CAN I DO WITH THESE BITS OF COLD CHICKEN?
I KNOW, I'LL USE MY TURKEY LEFT-OVERS RECIPE WITH CELERY
CUT CELERY INTO PIECES
I ALWAYS KEEP THE LEAVES FOR FLAVOURING
CHOP CHOP
JUST ENOUGH OIL TO COVER THE BOTTOM...
ADD: SALT, PEPPER + 1 CUP OF WATER
SHAKE
SHAKE TO MIX
COVER & SIMMER......
MEANWHILE I CAN PREPARE THE CHICKEN
MINCE THE BONED CHICKEN + 1 MEDIUM ONION + A FEW CELERY LEAVES...
FOR THIS AMOUNT OF MEAT (ABOUT 10 oz) 1 large egg SHOULD BE OKAY!
OH DEAR!
IT'S TOO SOFT TO HANDLE—I'LL ADD A SPOONFUL OF BREADCRUMBS
SHAPE MIXTURE INTO WALNUT-SHAPED BALLS
ROLL IN BREADCRUMBS
GENTLY FRY UNTIL GOLDEN
THEN LIFT...
AND THROW INTO casserole
Simmer for another 15 MINS. OR UNTIL CELERY IS TENDER
POUR sauce from casserole over dish of cooked potatoes
CHICKEN & CELERY SURROUND

DESSERTS SWEETS CAKES

☆ EVEN IF YOU'RE LIKE ME AND USUALLY EAT FRESH FRUIT FOR DESSERT—

☆ YOU STILL NEED A FEW RECIPES IN YOUR REPERTOIRE...

☆ SOME ARE JUST CLEVER IMPROVISATIONS

YA HEY!

OH BOY OH BOY

SUMMER FRUIT SALAD (CHEAT!)

BANANAS
STRAWBERRIES
ORANGES
JUICE OF LIME OR LEMON

THIS IS REALLY MY FAVOURITE MIXTURE...

START WITH SOME JUICE

PEEL AND SLICE THE BANANAS AND THROW THEM INTO THE JUICE IMMEDIATELY TO PREVENT DISCOLOURING

SHAKE THE BOWL

THEN ADD THE STRAWBERRIES THE ORANGES CUT INTO SLICES

ADD SUGAR TO TASTE (I DON'T) AND POP INTO FRIDGE

SERVE CHILLED WITH CREAM IF YOU DARE

WINTER FRUIT SALAD

☆FOR A SMALLER VERSION, JUST BUY ONE PACKET OF MIXED DRIED FRUIT YOU CAN GET AT THE SUPERMARKET TO WHICH YOU ADD SOME MORE APRICOTS FOR EXTRA TANG ——
THERE WILL BE PLENTY FOR SIX TO EIGHT PORTIONS

FRUIT ICES

I'VE RECENTLY STARTED MAKING FRUIT ICES — IT'S SO EASY, SUCH FUN AND SO DELICIOUS...

ADD: 8 OZ OF FRUIT TO A SYRUP MADE WITH 4 OZ SUGAR + 1 PINT OF WATER

SIMMER FOR A FEW MINUTES THEN LIQUIDISE & RETURN TO THE PAN

(IF YOU USE FRUIT WITH PIPS, SIEVE THROUGH A MUSLIN)

STIR FOR A FEW MINUTES & ADD THE JUICE OF A LEMON

NOW POUR INTO A WIDE BOWL

WHEN COLD POP INTO FREEZER (OR FREEZER COMPARTMENT OF THE FRIDGE SET AT ITS LOWEST)

AFTER ABOUT 1 HOUR WHISK THE MIXTURE

AT THIS STAGE YOU COULD ADD THE WHITE OF AN EGG STIFFLY BEATEN OR 2OZ WHIPPED CREAM (I PREFER TO LEAVE THESE OUT)

BACK INTO THE FREEZER & GIVE THE MIXTURE ANOTHER BEATING AFTER 20 MINUTES (APPROX.)

AND THEN TRANSFER IT INTO SMALLER CONTAINERS

I USE THOSE PLASTIC STRAWBERRY PUNNETS YOU GET FROM GREENGROCERS

PUT ON ORDINARY SHELF OF FRIDGE AT USUAL TEMPERATURE ABOUT 20 MINUTES BEFORE SERVING

BANANA FLAMBÉES

OH DEAR, I'VE DONE IT AGAIN!
I'VE PLANNED THE WHOLE
MEAL AND FORGOTTEN ALL
ABOUT THE SWEET——

WELL, THESE THREE
LARGE BANANAS
WILL BE ENOUGH
FOR FOUR PORTIONS
→

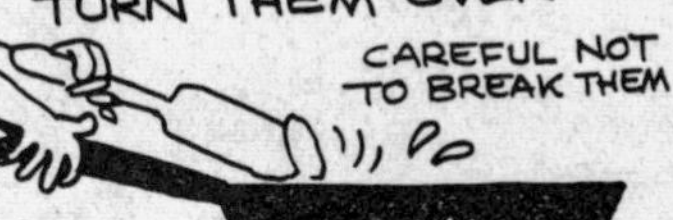

WHEN IT BUBBLES

GET THE BRANDY OR RUM

LONG SPOON

ONE TWO...

FOR THE THIRD SPOONFUL I WARM THE SPOON FIRST THEN ADD THE ALCOHOL

TO SET ALIGHT:
BE CAREFUL — GET HELP IF YOU ARE WORRIED

NO, I PREFER IT JUST AS IT IS — IT BRINGS BACK SUCH MEMORIES

DATE & BANANA DESSERT

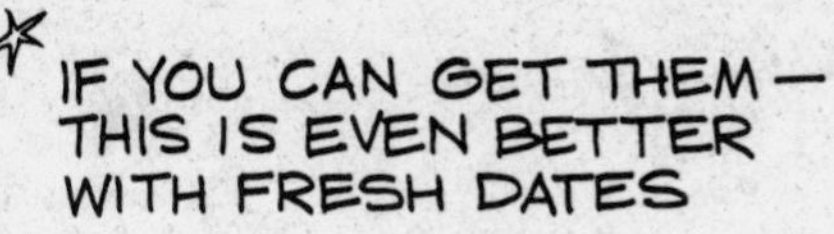

WASH THE DATES JUST BEFORE USE

(IF THEY'RE WET FOR ANY LENGTH OF TIME THEY TURN SOUR UGH!

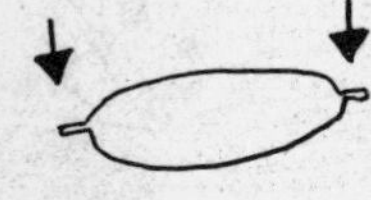

FIRST DISCARD THE TWO TIPS OF THE DATE

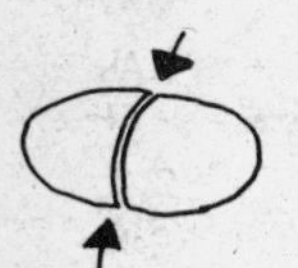

THEN SLIT THE PEEL ALL ROUND THE MIDDLE WITH A SHARP KNIFE

HOLD & TWIST AND THE PEEL WILL COME OFF

THEN STONE — AND PROCEED AS SHOWN ON THE OPPOSITE PAGE

ORANGE DESSERT (IN CARAMEL)

SHOULD YOU BE CAUGHT
NAPPING

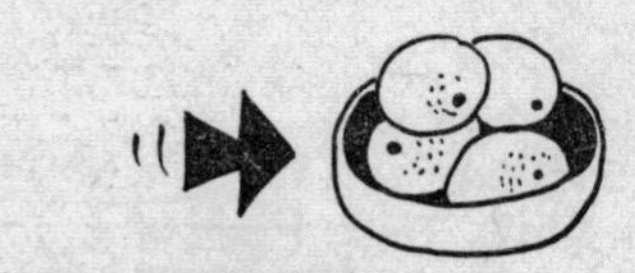

ALL YOU NEED IS
A FEW ORANGES

YOU'RE IN TOWN? —GREAT, DROP IN FOR A MEAL BUT YOU'LL HAVE TO TAKE POT LUCK!
I'M ALL RIGHT FOR THE MAIN COURSE—BUT THAT'S ALL I HAVE FOR DESSERT...
3 ORANGES
FOR FOUR PEOPLE
Well— with a bit of Imagination....
4 TABLESPOONS OF SUGAR 4 TABLESPOONS OF WATER JUICE OF ONE LEMON
LOW HEAT
THIS IS FOR THE CARAMEL
Meanwhile... WASH ORANGES—THEN
CUT ENDS & DISCARD
SCORE THE PEEL
AND REMOVE THE SEGMENTS
CUT PEEL INTO FINE STRIPS
THROW INTO FRYING PAN AND STIR
THE SUGAR IS ALL DISSOLVED NOW—LET'S COVER THE PAN...
CUT ORANGES INTO SLICES...
OH— I'VE GOT A LITTLE BRANDY
I'LL POUR IT ON —LOVELY STUFF
IT'S BEGINNING TO COLOUR NICELY— I MUST WATCH IT, DON'T LET IT BURN—NOW IT'S GOLDEN BROWN
I'LL POUR A CUP OF WATER IN— LET IT JUST THICKEN AGAIN...
POUR IT ALL OVER THE ORANGES AND POP INTO FRIDGE!
Mmm... SUZY— SOME POT LUCK!

MEHALABEYA (CORNFLOUR JELLY) A MIDDLE EASTERN DISH:

THIS IS AN EASY TO MAKE
AND VERY REFRESHING SWEET
YOU CAN VARY THE PROPORTIONS
OF MILK & WATER
AS YOU LIKE — i.e: HALF & HALF
FOR A LIGHTER ONE AND YOU
CAN ALSO DO IT WITH MILK ONLY

*OTHER FLAVOURS ROSE OR ORANGE
BLOSSOM WATER
& GARNISH WITH ROUGHLY CHOPPED
ROASTED NUTS

SUTLACH (RICE PUDDING CARAMEL)

LET ME SEE — HOW MUCH SHALL I MAKE FOR 6?
GROUND RICE
3 OZ GROUND RICE TO 2 PINTS OF MILK
BLEND THE RICE WITH SOME OF THE COLD MILK WHILE BOILING THE REST...
MILK TO BOIL
RICE
NOW
STIR THE BOILING MILK INTO THE MIXTURE...
AND THAT GOES BACK INTO THE PAN ON A LOW HEAT
STIR UNTIL IT THICKENS TO A DOUBLE CREAM CONSISTENCY
NOW ADD 2 TABLESPOONS OF SUGAR...
... AND POUR INTO OVEN PROOF DISH
NOW I CAN GET ON WITH THE caramel
LOW HEAT
8oz SUGAR
3 TABLESPOONS WATER
A SQUEEZE OF LEMON JUICE
CAREFUL NOW — IT'S BEGINNING TO COLOUR — I WANT IT A DARKISH CARAMEL BROWN
(DON'T BURN IT THOUGH!)
ADD ABOUT HALF A TEACUP OF WATER
FIZZZ
AND STIR
OFF THE STOVE!
POUR CARAMEL OVER THE DISH AND GIVE IT A STIR
IT'S A BEAUTIFUL BROWN MARBLE EFFECT....
POP INTO OVEN 350° (GAS MARK 4) FOR ABOUT 45 MINS.
COOL BEFORE PUTTING INTO THE FRIDGE FOR A FEW HOURS...
P.S.. IT'S ALSO NICE EATEN HOT...

RAISIN PUDDING

ALL YOU NEED TO DO IS SIMMER 4 OZ RAISINS IN ½ PINT WATER

MEANWHILE CRUSH 4 OZ DIGESTIVE BISCUITS

PUT THEM IN A CLOTH & BASH IT WITH A ROLLING PIN

CRUNCH

SQUASH 2 OZ BUTTER INTO THE CRUMBLED BISCUITS

TRANSFER INTO A SERVING BOWL & PACK TIGHTLY AT THE BOTTOM

NOW GO BACK TO THE SIMMERING RAISINS & ADD 2 TABLESPOONS OF BROWN SUGAR

STIR & ADD A DESSERT-SPOONFUL OF CORNFLOUR

AND POUR IT OVER THE BISCUIT MIXTURE

WHEN COOL

POP INTO THE FRIDGE

SERVE WITH CREAM

IT'S DELICIOUS, BUT I THINK I'D RATHER HAVE MORE BISCUITS AND LESS RAISINS, SUZY

YOU CAN OF COURSE — IT DEPENDS ON HOW SWEET YOUR TOOTH IS

WITH SUCH RICH SWEETS
I LIKE TO USE INSTEAD
OF CREAM ONLY —
A MIXTURE OF
CURD CHEESE
& CREAM
(WHIP 4 OZ CURD
+ 2 TABLESPOONS
CREAM)
THE SLIGHTLY SOUR TASTE
GOES VERY WELL WITH THE
SWEETNESS OF THE RAISINS
CURD

CHOCOLATE MOUSSE

HOW I LIKE TO USE CHOCOLATE—

TOMORROW'S SWEET IS EVERYONE'S FAVOURITE—ESPECIALLY MINE!
IT'S SO EASY TO MAKE
8 OZ PLAIN CHOCOLATE
6 LARGE EGGS
MELT 6 OZ CHOCOLATE WITH A LITTLE MILK
WATER
MEDIUM HEAT
SEPARATE YOLKS FROM WHITES
CAREFUL NOW— THERE SHOULD BE NO TRACE OF YOLK IN THE WHITES...
THE CHOCOLATE IS MELTED NOW—
SO TAKE IT OFF THE STOVE
BEAT YOLKS
AND WHITES STIFF
NOW BLEND THE CHOCOLATE WELL INTO THE YOLKS
FOLD IN THE EGG WHITES INTO THE MIXTURE...
NOT TOO MUCH AT A TIME!
GENTLY GENTLY DOES IT!...
WIPE CLEAN THE SIDES OF THE BOWL
GRATE THE REST OF THE CHOCOLATE TO COVER TOP
I'VE GOT SOME NICE SPONGE FINGERS TO PUT AROUND THE EDGE—
NOW I POP IT INTO THE FRIDGE UNTIL TOMORROW!

BASIC SHORT PASTRY (SWEET)

YOU CAN OF COURSE, USE YOUR FAVOURITE SHORT PASTRY... OR BUY PUFF PASTRY. BOUGHT PASTRY IS USUALLY VERY GOOD VALUE — BUT OF COURSE IF YOU'RE A VERY SKILFUL PASTRYMAKER YOUR OWN WOULD BE MUCH BETTER AND MUCH MORE FUN...

TRY MINE ➡

4 OZ BUTTER
WITH
1 TABLESPOON
OF SUGAR
WHEN CREAMY
ADD 1 EGG &
CONTINUE BEATING
THEN 2 TABLESPOONS
OF OIL
OIL
10oz
PLAIN
FLOUR
MIX 2
FLAT
TEA SPOONS
OF BAKING
POWDER
WITH 10oz
FLOUR
NOW POUR
THIS
INTO THE
MIXTURE
IN THE
BOWL
AND STIR
UNTIL THE
DOUGH COMES
OFF THE SIDE
OF THE
BOWL
GATHER
THE
DOUGH
IN YOUR
HANDS
KEEP IN A
COOL PLACE
FOR 10 MINUTES
FOR EASIER
HANDLING
10" FLAN DISH
YOU DON'T ROLL THIS
PASTRY IT'S TOO
CRUMBLY — YOU
FLATTEN IT WITH
YOUR HAND
PUSH THE DOUGH
UP THE SIDES OF
THE
DISH
IF YOU'RE COOKING
IT BLIND SLIT THE
DOUGH WITH A
SHARP KNIFE
LINE THE PASTRY
WITH GREASE-PROOF
PAPER & WEIGHT DOWN
WITH DRIED BEANS
I ALWAYS KEEP THESE
BEANS IN A JAR & USE
THEM TIME & TIME AGAIN
OVEN PRE-
HEATED
GAS 4 350°F
IT TAKES ABOUT
40 MINUTES —
BUT DO CHECK & PUT
IT BACK IF NECESSARY
WITHOUT THE PAPER
LINING & BEANS
MIND —
IT'S HOT!
WHEN COLD IT'S
READY TO TAKE
IN THE FILLINGS
SEE FOLLOWING
PAGES FOR
FILLINGS

* FRUIT FLANS
* TARTS
* TARTLETS

VARIATIONS ON A THEME

KITCHEN ←

WITH A PASTRY BASE

A GOOD CRÈME PÂTISSIÈRE
SOME FRESH FRUIT
& A FRUIT SAUCE

THE PERMUTATIONS ARE INFINITE

SEE FOLLOWING PAGES...

☆ TAKE A PRE-COOKED PASTRY CASE

LINE IT WITH CRÈME PÂTISSIÈRE
COVER IT WITH FRUIT
STRAWBERRIES ☆ APRICOTS
RASPBERRIES, PEACHES ETC.

FOR A REAL PROFESSIONAL FINISH COVER WITH A GLOSSY FRUIT SAUCE

☆ EXAMPLES:

LIQUIDISE 4OZ RASPBERRIES WITH 2OZ SUGAR

BRING TO THE BOIL — LOWER THE HEAT & ADD A DESSERTSPOONFUL OF ARROWROOT

STIR FOR A COUPLE OF MINUTES
ADD SOME LEMON JUICE

WHEN COOL POUR OVER THE TART & CHILL

CRÈME PÂTISSIÈRE

ORANGE FLAN

USING THE BASIC PASTRY ON PAGE 160
(DO NOT PRE-COOK IT)
10"
FOR THE FILLING LIQUIDISE
2 LARGE EGGS
ADD A GLASSFUL OF SUGAR
+ 2oz MELTED BUTTER
SCRUB ORANGE
CUT IT TO REMOVE PIPS
NOW THROW INTO THE LIQUIDISER
IF YOU DON'T HAVE A LIQUIDISER USE THE GRATED RIND OF THE ORANGE & THE JUICE
NOW WHISK IT INTO THE MIXTURE
POUR THE WHOLE MIXTURE INTO PASTRY CASE
POP INTO A PRE-HEATED OVEN GAS 4 350°F
IT TAKES ABOUT 45 MINUTES
I'LL LEAVE IT A TINY BIT LONGER — IT SHOULD BE A GOLDEN COLOUR ALL OVER

OR TRY 4 OZ DRIED APRICOTS
SOAKED IN A GLASS OF WATER

THEN THROW
THE LOT INTO
THE MIXTURE

HAZELNUT SHORTCAKE

WHEN COLD
THESE ARE NICE
TO KEEP
IN A TIN...
cakes
IN A PLAINER VERSION
YOU DON'T USE
HAZELNUTS
BUT FLOUR ONLY
(10 oz)
hmmmmmm
Cakes
EITHER WAY
WATCH THE KIDS!

I SOMETIMES GET CARRIED AWAY WITH DATES!

4oz FAT
(BUTTER OR MARGARINE)
8oz Flour
8oz PACKET stoned DATES
I ALSO NEED SOME ICING SUGAR
IT'S AN ORDINARY SHORT PASTRY—BUT I PREFER WORKING THE FLOUR & FAT WITH A FORK
INSTEAD OF RUBBING IT WITH THE FINGERS
*ONE TABLESPOON OF ICING SUGAR
IT'S NICE & CRUMBLY, NOW I ADD THE SUGAR* AND ENOUGH COLD WATER TO BIND THE PASTRY
COLD WATER
PASTRY INTO FRIDGE WHILE PREPARING FILLING
CUT UP THE DATES
LOW HEAT
ADD JUST A LITTLE WATER TO MELT THE DATES INTO A PASTE
RIGHT!
THAT'LL SPREAD EASILY—NOW LET IT COOL
CUT PASTRY IN HALF
(IT'S EASIER TO WORK IN TWO PIECES)
ROLL EACH HALF INTO A RECTANGLE
14"
7"
SPREAD HALF THE DATE PASTE ON TO THE PASTRY
NOW ROLL IT
VERY GENTLY,,
JUST LIKE A SWISS ROLL
GENTLY FLATTEN THE ROLL THEN CUT DIAGONALLY ACCROSS!
ABOUT 1 INCH
PINCH HOLES WITH TWEEZERS
YOU SHOULD GET ABOUT 2 DOZEN PIECES...
POP INTO A PRE-HEATED OVEN 350 OR GAS MARK 4
AFTER ABOUT 25 MINS
CHECK —— THE TOP HAS TO REMAIN WHITE
LIFT
AND YOU KNOW THEY'RE DONE WHEN THE UNDERSIDE BEGINS TO COLOUR
COOLING RACK
SPRINKLE WITH ICING SUGAR!

MARBLED CAKE

THIS IS THE SORT OF CAKE THAT'S ALWAYS NICE TO HAVE HANDY — YOU CAN MAKE IT PLAIN OR VANILLA FLAVOURED OR WITH A HANDFUL OF RAISINS, SULTANAS OR WITH CHOCOLATE.

CHOCOLATE GÂTEAU (SOFT CENTRE)

Mmmmmm m ITS SO CREAMY
—— YES, IT HAS TO BE QUITE
MOIST INSIDE. THAT'S WHY YOU
MUST NEVER CUT IT
UNLESS IT IS
QUITE, QUITE,
COLD

OH BOY

HAZELNUT GÂTEAU

BEAT 4oz SUGAR & 4oz BUTTER
WHEN CREAMY ADD 2 LARGE EGGS

GO ON BEATING & ADD ½ PINT MILK

PRE HEAT OVEN REGULO 4 350°F

MIX 4oz BREADCRUMBS +1 HEAPED TEASPOON OF BAKING POWDER

+4oz GROUND ROASTED HAZELNUTS (SEE PAGE 168)
+ A TEASPOON CINNAMON

MIX WELL

STIR IN THE EGG, BUTTER & SUGAR MIXTURE

TRANSFER THE LOT INTO A BUTTERED TIN

7" CAKE TIN

☆ POP INTO OVEN

IT SHOULD TAKE AN HOUR BUT CHECK AFTER ABOUT 50 MINUTES

☆ (BECAUSE NO TWO OVENS ARE THE SAME)

NOW TEST WITH A SKEWER

THE SKEWER MUST COME OUT ABSOLUTELY CLEAN

WHEN DONE COOL ON A COOLING RACK

DECORATE AS YOU FANCY ☆

A FEW IDEAS ON PAGE 178

GROUND ALMOND GÂTEAU

A VARIATION ON THE PREVIOUS ONE

INSTEAD OF HAZELNUT I USED 4 OZ OF GROUND ALMOND. INSTEAD OF CINNAMON — I FLAVOURED THIS CAKE WITH A TABLESPOONFUL OF GRATED ORANGE RIND AND — WHY NOT TWO TABLESPOONS OF Brandy

SOME QUICK & EASY IDEAS...
GRATED CHOCOLATE
COARSE GRATING
FINE GRATING
(POWDERED)
OVER A SIEVE
YOU CAN MAKE A PATTERN IF YOU PUT A PAPER DOILY ON THE CAKE FIRST AND THEN DUST WITH ICING SUGAR

...TO DECORATE CAKES
ADD GRILLED
(WHOLE) HAZELNUTS
OR ALMONDS ARRANGED
IN A PATTERN
OR JUST A
SPRINKLING
OF MIXED
CHOPPED
NUTS

weights and measures

Conversion Table

LIQUID MEASURES

BRITISH

1 quart	=	2 pints	=	40 fl oz
1 pint	=	4 gills	=	20 fl oz
½ pint	=	2 gills		
		or one cup	=	10 fl oz
¼ pint	=	8 tablespoons	=	5 fl oz
		1 tablespoon	=	just over ½ fl oz
		1 dessertspoon	=	⅓ fl oz
		1 teaspoon	=	⅙ fl oz

METRIC

1 litre = 10 decilitres (dl) = 100 centilitres (cl) = 1000 millilitres (ml)

AMERICAN

1 quart	=	2 pints	=	32 fl oz
1 pint	=	2 cups	=	16 fl oz
		1 cup	=	8 fl oz
		1 tablespoon	=	⅓ fl oz
		1 teaspoon	=	⅙ fl oz

Approx. equivalents

BRITISH	METRIC
1 quart	1·1 litre
1 pint	6 dl
½ pint	3 dl
¼ pint (1 gill)	1·5 dl
1 tablespoon	15 ml
1 dessertspoon	10 ml
1 teaspoon	5 ml

METRIC	BRITISH
1 litre	35 fl oz
½ litre (5 dl)	18 fl oz
¼ litre (2·5 dl)	9 fl oz
1 dl	3½ fl oz

BRITISH	AMERICAN
1 quart	2½ pints
1 pint	1¼ pints
½ pint	10 fl oz (1¼ cups)
¼ pint (1 gill)	5 fl oz
1 tablespoon	1½ tablespoons
1 dessertspoon	1 tablespoon
1 teaspoon	⅓ fl oz

AMERICAN	BRITISH
1 quart	1½ pints + 3 tbs (32 fl oz)
1 pint	¾ pint + 2 tbs (16 fl oz)
1 cup	½ pint − 2 tbs (8 fl oz)

SOLID MEASURES

BRITISH

16 oz = 1 lb

METRIC

1000 grammes = 1 kilogramme

Approx. equivalents

BRITISH	METRIC
1 lb (16 oz)	400 grammes
½ lb (8 oz)	200 g
¼ lb (4 oz)	100 g
1 oz	25 g

METRIC	BRITISH
1 kilo (1000g)	2 lb 3 oz
½ kilo (500g)	1 lb 2 oz
¼ kilo (250g)	9 oz
100g	3½ oz

TABLE OF TEMPERATURE EQUIVALENTS FOR OVEN THERMOSTAT MARKINGS

Present Scale Fahrenheit	*Gas*	*Recommended Conversion to Centigrade Scale*
225°F	*Mark* ¼	110°C
250°F	½	130°C
275°F	1	140°C
300°F	2	150°C
325°F	3	170°C
350°F	4	180°C
375°F	5	190°C
400°F	6	200°C
425°F	7	220°C
450°F	8	230°C
475°F	9	240°C

index